BASKETBALL

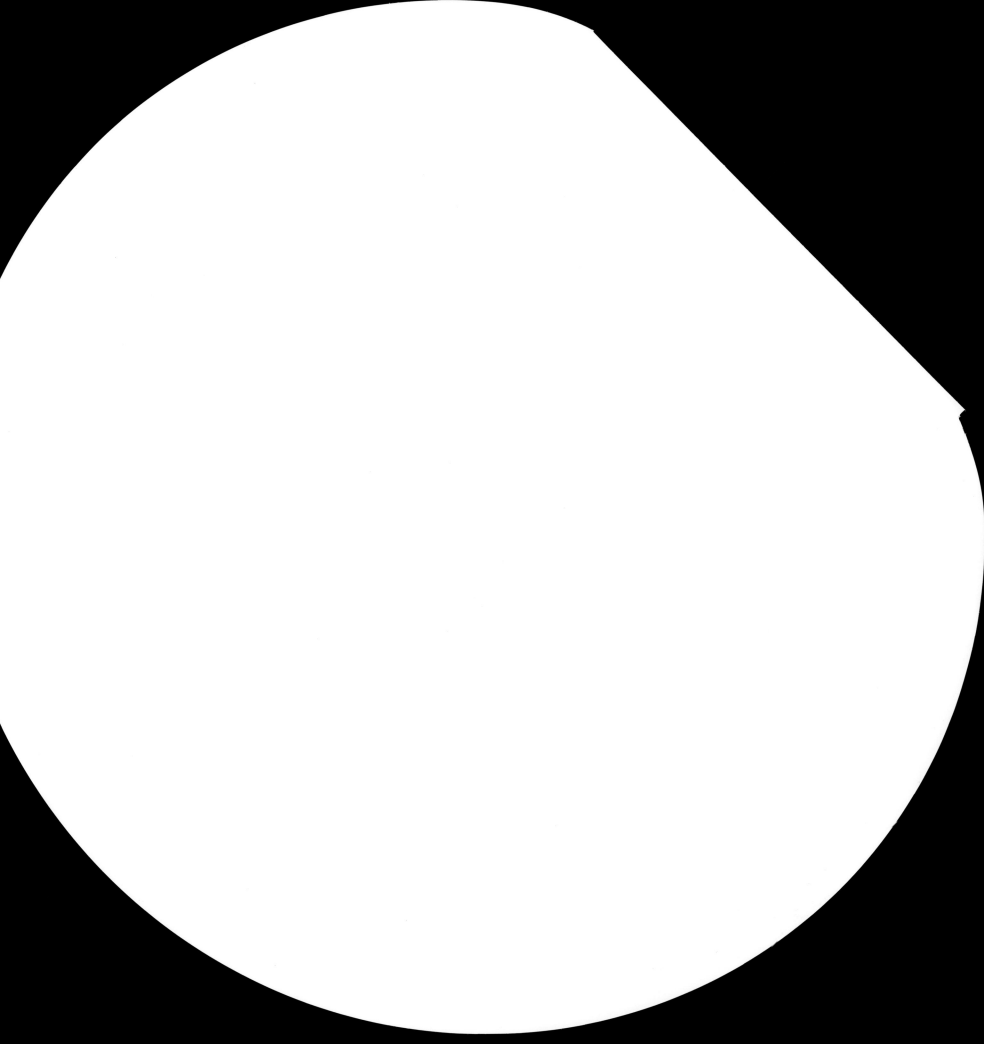

BASKETBALL

MURRAY BOOKS

MURRAY BOOKS

TOOTS™

"Think out of the square"

First published in 2007
by Murray Books (Australia)
Reprinted in 2008, 2009 and 2010
www.murraybooks.com

Design and Production: Peter Murray

The author and publisher have made every effort to ensure the information contained in this book was correct at the time of going to press and accept no responsibility for any loss, injury or inconvenience sustained by any person using this book.

All images: Getty Images

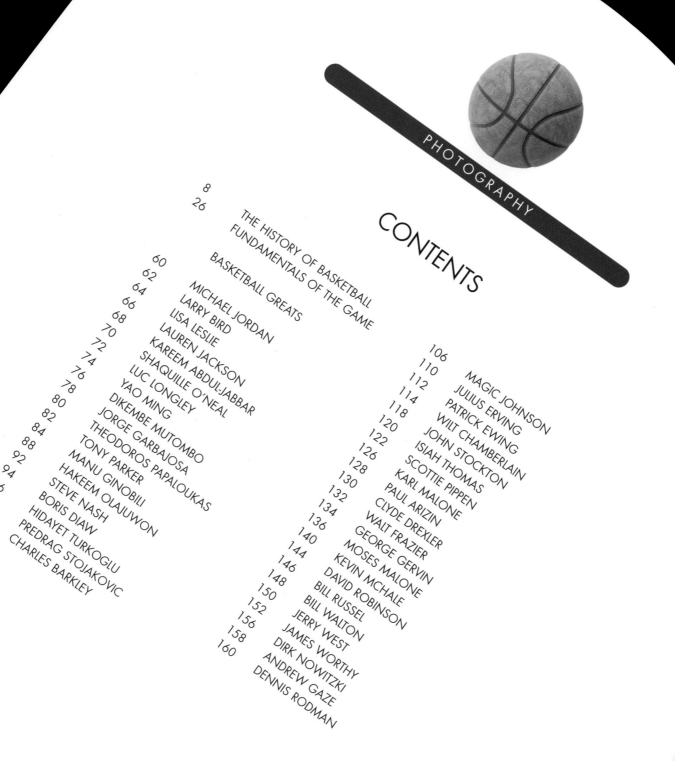

CONTENTS

INTRODUCTION

Basketball is a sport that is played between two teams of five active players who aim to score points against the opposing team by throwing a ball through a 10-ft high basket, which is fixed at both ends of a rectangular court. The team who has possession of the ball is said to be the offence and their sole aim is to try and get their ball down their end of the court and into their designated basket. The team who does not have possession of the ball is said to be the defensive team. The role of the defence is to try and prevent the other team from scoring points and win back possession of the basket so that they in turn can attack and score at their basket.

There are various rules and regulations that govern how the sport is played. Officiated by designated umpires or referees, certain restrictions are placed on players and teams so that play is kept orderly and fair for all involved. These include limitations on the playing area, elements of time and various offensive and defensive actions, such as the number of personal and team fouls. Specifications apply also to how points are scored, how much time a team can have possession of a ball and how many players can be on the court per team at any one time.

Originally developed and played in the United States in the late 19th century, today basketball is one of the most widely viewed and played sports in the world. It enjoys immense popularity in the United States but also in many European and Austral-Asian countries. The most popular and well-known professional league is the National Basketball Association based in the USA. Backed by huge commercial entities and corporate companies, teams in the NBA generate massive following by employing some of the most talented and highly skilled players, not only from in the United States but from all over the world. The players are paid mega-bucks to not only help their teams win, but also to please the crowd with flashy offensive moves, spectacular shots and slam-dunks and impressive defensive performances.

6

HISTORY OF BASKETBALL

Canadian born, Dr. James Naismith (pictured right) invented the sport of basketball in 1891. Born in the small town of Ramsay, near Almonte, Ontario, Naismith attended McGill University in Montreal, Quebec and then went on to serve as the University's Athletic Director before relocating to the Young Men's Christian Association (YMCA) Training School in Springfield, Massachusetts, USA. Under the instruction of the Head of Physical Education, Naismith was given the task of providing an "athletic distraction" for a bored and unruly class by inventing a game that would keep his students entertained and occupied as well as physically fit during the long, harsh Massachusetts winters. Given a two week deadline, Naismith went about designing a sport that was not only suitable to play indoors in a relatively small space, but one that relied just as much on skill and mental intelligence as it did on strength and physical exertion.

After initially rejecting other ideas as too rough or unable to be confined to a closed-in gymnasium, Dr. Naismith created a sport that combined various elements of outdoor games such as soccer and lacrosse with the concept of the children's game, 'duck-on-a-rock,' which

involved attempting to knock a "duck" off the top of a boulder with another rock from a distance of about 20ft. After conceiving the idea, Naismith devised a list of rules for an orderly and simple ball game. The aim of this new sport was for a player to throw a ball into a designated peach basket, which were nailed onto a 10ft (3.05m) elevated track at each end of the YMCA gymnasium, in order to score a point for their team. Whichever team got the ball into the basket the most times and thus the most points, won the game.

The first rules of Basketball as set out by Dr. James Naismith:

- The ball may be thrown in any direction with one or both hands.
- The ball may be batted in any direction with one or both hands but never with the fist.
- A player cannot run with the ball. The player must throw it from the spot on which he catches it, allowance to be made for a man who catches the ball when running at a good speed if he tries to stop.
- The ball must be held in or between the hands; the arms or body must not be used for holding it.

8

HISTORY OF BASKETBALL

- No shouldering, holding, pushing, tripping, or striking in any way of an opponent; the first infringement of this rule by any player shall count as a foul, the second shall disqualify him until the next goal is made, or, if there was evident intent to injure the person, for the whole of the game, no substitute allowed.
- A foul is striking at the ball with the fist; violation of Rules 3,4, and such as described in Rule 5.
- If either side makes three consecutive fouls, it shall count a goal for the opponents (consecutive means making without the opponents in the mean time making a foul).
- A goal shall be made when the ball is thrown or batted from the grounds into the basket and stays there, providing those defending the goal do not touch or disturb the goal. If the ball rests on the edges, and the opponent moves the basket, it shall count as a goal.
- When the ball goes out of bounds, it shall be thrown into the field of play by the person first touching it. In case of a dispute, the umpire shall throw it straight into the field. The thrower-in is allowed five seconds; if he holds it longer, it shall go to the opponent. If any side persists in delaying the game, the umpire shall call a foul on that side.

- The umpire shall be judge of the men and shall note the fouls and notify the referee when three consecutive fouls have been made. He shall have power to disqualify men according to Rule 5.
- The referee shall be judge of the ball and shall decide when the ball is in play, in bounds, to which side it belongs, and shall keep the time. He shall decide when a goal has been made, and keep account of the goals with any other duties that are usually performed by a referee.
- The time shall be two 15-minute halves, with five minutes' rest between.
- The side making the most goals in that time shall be declared the winner. In case of a draw, the game may, by agreement of the captains, be continued until another goal is made.

Note: These original rules were published in January 1892 in the Springfield College school newspaper, The Triangle.

The first official game of 'basket ball' took place on the January 20 1892, in the Springfield, Massachusetts YMCA Training School gymnasium. Naismith's class of 18 was divided into two teams and they soon set

BASKETBALL

HISTORY OF BASKETBALL

about playing the game with nine a side on the 50ft x 35ft court. The first game was played using a soccer ball, which they attempted to throw into the peach baskets at each end of the gymnasium, hence the name 'basketball'. Unlike modern basketball nets, the original peach basket had a sealed bottom, thus when points were scored the umpire would have to get down from his chair and use a long stick to poke the ball out of the basket. Luckily for the umpire, the first game was a low-scoring affair with the final score of the game 1-0. The lone point was scored by William Chase 25ft away from the basket, a half-court shot given the size of the court.

involving a male college basketball team took place in Pittsburgh area town of Beaver Falls, when a team from Geneva College defeated nearby New Brighton YMCA.

The early 1890's also saw the game of basketball spread to other parts of the globe. Naismith's original class of students, many of whom were from abroad, helped spread the game across the world when they returned to their home countries. The YMCA also helped promote the new sport overseas. C.J. Proctor, the then president of the Birkenhead YMCA, first introduced basketball in England between March 1892 and January 1893. In 1893, the first game of basketball played in Europe took place in Paris, France.

Around the same time, women were also introduced to basketball, although it was met with great opposition in some circles, with many believing the sport was too 'manly' for women to play. At the all-female Smith's College, physical education teacher Senda Bereson modified Naismith's rules to make the sport more "acceptable" for female players, emphasising teamwork and cooperation between players rather than competition. In order to minimise excessive running, the female version of the rules required the court

The Development of Basketball

Basketball quickly became a popular men's sport. The YMCA network and associated recreation centres began promoting the sport and interest and participation in the sport quickly spread through out the United States and Canada. Just two months after the first official game, the Central YMCA and the Armory Hill YMCA played in the first competitive game, with the final score 2-2. On April 8, 1893, the first recorded game

HISTORY OF BASKETBALL

to be divided into three separate zones. three of the nine players from each team had to remain in one of the three zones at all times with the players not allowed to leave their designated zone. In addition, a player could only hold onto the ball for three seconds and dribble the ball three times before passing, which encouraged team input rather than an individual contribution. The players also had to wear skirts to keep their "woman-like" appearance. On March 21, 1893, the first official women's collegiate basketball game took place between the Smith sophomores and freshman teams, in what is now known as the Alumnae Gymnasium. Played in front of an all-female crowd with no males allowed in the stadium, the freshman class managed to beat their seniors 5 to 4. That same year, other colleges including Mount Holyoke and Sophie Newcomb College also introduced basketball to their female students.

coach to have lost more games than won, with a 55-60 record, he played an integral role in establishing an intercollegiate basketball competition. Basketball proved to be the perfect interscholastic sport due to its simple equipment and personnel requirements and by the mid 1890's it was a well-entrenched sport within several high schools and colleges across the USA and Canada. On February 9, 1895, the first male intercollegiate game was played featuring the Minnesota State School of Agriculture (now the University of Minnesota, St. Paul campus), who defeated Hamline College 9-3. Whilst female participation in the sport was still limited, the first women's intercollegiate basketball game was held the following year on April 4, 1896 when Stanford College defeated Berkeley College, 2-1.

The first professional league was formed in the United States, in 1898. The competition included six teams and lasted six years. By the beginning of the 20th Century, so many colleges in the United States were fielding basketball teams that leagues began to form and various colleges including the University of Chicago, Columbia University, University of Utah, the U.S. Naval Academy

Naismith remained actively involved in the development of the game after his invention and was particularly instrumental in the growth of college basketball. He became the head coach at the University of Kansas and although he is the only Kansas basketball

HISTORY OF BASKETBALL

and Dartmouth College began sponsoring of basketball to spread to other parts of the men's games. Basketball was also being played world. Basketball in Europe in particular was internationally. In 1909, the Russian club influenced greatly by American forces during Mayak played against a visiting YMCA team, and after the war and many European believed to be the very first international countries as a result began to play basketball basketball game. for the first time. In places where basketball had already been introduced, such as England,

However, even though the YMCA initially local rules were altered slightly and the style of encouraged the sport, within a decade the game of the game became more like the American association was discouraging the game of version of the game. British basketball in basketball. Rough play, numerous injuries and particular was greatly influenced during this rowdy crowds began to detract from the period and YMCA clubs across England YMCA's primary mission of a team sport that developed the game with added flavour. inspired mental as well as physical Rules, however, continued to vary according conditioning. Despite this, other amateur to the country in which the game was played, sports clubs, colleges and professional bodies which continued to be the case for a great quickly filled the void and began competing number of years. for control over the rules of the game. In 1910, the Intercollegiate Athletic Association, the After the war, the development of predecessor of the National Collegiate Athletic basketball competition gained momentum Association (NCAA), was created to control once again. In 1919, the first international the rules of the game and organise a structured basketball tournament, the Inter-Allied league. Games, was held in Paris. The competition was won by the USA, defeating France and Italy. In The advent of World War I meant that the USA hundreds of men's professional basketball lost a great deal of its initial basketball teams soon formed in towns and momentum and although many games were cities all over the country. But despite the IAA, played during the war years, the development there was little organisation of the game. of the game was limited. However, it did Players jumped from team to team and various provide an opportunity for the American-style

16

HISTORY OF BASKETBALL

leagues formed and folded. Barnstorming teams were formed, which travelled nationally from town to town playing in up to 200 games a year in front of primarily small crowds, including two all African-American teams, the still existing Harlem Globetrotters (right) and the New York Renaissance Five. Both teams were unable to join any professional leagues at the time due to racial discrimination, despite the Renaissance Five compiling a win / loss record of 112-8 during the 1932 -33 season and winning a total of 88 consecutive games, a feat that has never been matched by a professional basketball team.

and in 1926, the Amateur Athletic Union hosted the first national women's basketball championship, played according to the men's rules. By the late 1920's women's basketball teams had been created all over the nation, giving rise to famous athletes such as Babe Didrikson of the Golden Cyclones and the All American Red Heads Team who played against various men's teams, using men's rules.

Women's basketball was more ordered and controlled, even though female participation in the sport was still frowned upon by many. The National Women's Basketball Committee created the *Executive Committee on Basket Ball Rules* in 1905, which made it compulsory to have six to nine players per side and 11 officials. In 1924 the International Women's Sports Federation, which campaigned for a greater inclusion of females in sport, created a formal women's basketball competition. A year later, 37 women's high school varsity basketball or state tournaments had been held

In 1932 the Fédération Internationale de Basketball Amateur (FIBA), was formed to govern international basketball competition and define the global rules of the game, the equipment specifications and the facilities required. FIBA initially only oversaw amateur players and had eight founding nations: Argentina, Czechoslovakia, Greece, Italy, Latvia, Portugal, Romania and Switzerland. It later dropped the 'Amateur' and became known simply as the International Basketball Federation but retained FIBA as an abbreviation.

Two years later in 1934, the first college tournament in America was staged in New York's Madison Square Garden and as a result, male college basketball began to attract

18

HISTORY OF BASKETBALL

heightened interest. The first men's national championship event in America, the National Association of Intercollegiate Athletics (NAIA) tournament was organised in 1937 and in 1938 the first national championship for NCAA teams, the National Invitation Tournament in New York was staged. In the 1940's and early 1950's, betting scandals unsettled college basketball and many players were accused of match fixing and point shaving. As a result, the National Invitation Tournament loss support to the NCAA tournament.

Although an exhibition match was played at the 1904 Los Angeles Olympics, basketball was not actually included as an Olympic sport until the 1936 Berlin Olympic Games. The United States has, since, dominated Olympic basketball ever winning all but fourOlympic titles since it was included in the games. In 1948, the FIBA congress decided to organise a world championship every four years, between the Olympic tournaments and Championship for men was held in Buenos Aires, Argentina. FIBA limited the number of participating teams to ten; the three best teams at the preceding Olympic Games, the two best teams from Asia, Europe and South America, plus the organising country, which

automatically qualified. However, as no Asian team could find the funds to make the journey, the competition was opened to two neighbouring European teams; Spain and Yugoslavia. With the added support of the home-crowd, Argentina took the first championship title after defeating the USA 64 – 50 in the final.

Three years later, in 1953 the first FIBA World Championship for Women was held in Chile. It was not established as a consistent four-year cycle until 1967 and in 1983, the schedule was changed so that it would be held in even numbered non-Olympic years, which FIBA had imposed on the men's tournament in 1970. Russia and the USA have dominated the competition since its inception, with Brazil and Australia (in 2006) the only other countries to win the women's title. In 1976, women's basketball was also added to the Olympics with teams from Brazil and Australia again rivalling the American and Soviet/Russian squads.

On June the 6th, 1946 the Basketball Association for America (BAA) was formed by the owners of the major sports arenas in the Northeast and Midwest of the United States, including Madison Square Garden in New York City. The BAA was created to coordinate

HISTORY OF BASKETBALL

the top professional teams and provide a structured league for men's basketball, including governing the existing rules and introducing a few new regulations. Although there had been earlier attempts at professional basketball leagues, including the American Basketball League (ABL) and the National Basketball League (NBL), the BAA was the first league to endeavour to play mainly in large arenas in major cities.

Beginning with 11 teams, the first game was played in Toronto, Canada between the Toronto Huskies and the New York Knickerbockers on November 1, 1946. Three years later, the BAA agreed to merge with the NBL and the new league became known as the National Basketball Association (NBA). This expanded the league to include 17 franchises distributed within a mix of large and small cities across America. In 1950, the NBA consolidated to 11 franchises. This continued until 1954 when the league reached its smallest of only eight franchises. This included the Knickerbockers, Celtics Warriors, Lakers, Royals / Kings, Pistons, Hawks and Nationals / 76ers, all of which are still in operation today.

The 1950's also saw for the very first time a racially integrated league with the inclusion of many African-American players into several teams, including Chuck Cooper, Nat "Sweetwater" Clifton (pictured right) with the Boston Celtics, with the New York Knicks and Earl Lloyd with the Washington Capitols. In 1954, the 24-second shot clock was also introduced, which encouraged shooting and prevented games from stalling or being held-up by an offence team for too long. The rule, which still applies to today's game, stipulated that if a team did not attempt to score a field goal within 24 seconds of obtaining the ball, play would be stopped and the ball would be given to the opposing team.

During the 1960's, the NBA continued to strengthen with the addition of its first expansion franchises and the relocation of large franchises. Minneapolis Lakers to Los Angeles, the Philadelphia Warriors to San Francisco and the Syracuse Nationals to Philadelphia. In 1967, the American Basketball Association emerged as an external rival league and briefly threatened the NBA's dominance. The two leagues engaged in a bidding war for talent both trying to out do the other by securing major stars. Following the 1976 season, the rival leagues merged and the four ABA

HISTORY OF BASKETBALL

franchises were added to the existing NBA teams, resulting in a total of 22 franchises. The merger also introduced the ABA's innovative three-point field goal line to the NBA in 1979, which opened up the game and made for spectacular shooting. It was also the beginning of a long period of significant growth in spectator and fan support in the NBA through the country and the world. This was sparked by the rise of rookies Larry Bird and Magic Johnson to the league. Not long after, in 1984, the famous Michael Jordan entered the league with the Chicago Bulls. His spectacular style of play and extraordinary talent spurred an unprecedented interest in the NBA. Leading the Bulls to six NBA titles (1991, 1992, 1993, 1996, 1997 and 1998), Jordan propelled the NBA and basketball in general into the world spotlight and lead to the globalisation of the league.

A growing number of NBA star players began coming from other countries. Initially many of these recruits played NCAA basketball to enhance their skills before entering the league. However, recently an increasing number have moved directly from playing elsewhere in the world to starring in the NBA, such as 2002 NBA Rookie of the Year and 2006 World Championships MVP Pau Gasol of Spain, first pick in the 2002 NBA Draft Yao Ming of China, Eurobasket 2005 MVP and the 2007 NBA MVP Dirk Nowitzki of Germany and 2004 Olympic Tournament MVP Manu Ginobili of Argentina. Today, the NBA is the top professional basketball league in the world in terms of popularity, salaries, talent and level of competition, with players coming from all over the world. It has now reached 30 franchises, 29 of which are based in the United States and one team located in Canada. The NBA is now televised in 212 nations and in 42 languages and continues to evolve as one of the premier sports leagues in the world.

In 1996, the Women's National Basketball Association (WNBA) was created as the female counterpart to the NBA and was the first female competition to receive full backing from the men's league. It began its first season on June 21, 1997 with eight teams and the first game was held in Los Angeles, between the New York Liberty and the Los Angeles Sparks. Star players Rebecca Lobo, Lisa Leslie and Sheryl Swoopes gradually helped increase the popularity of the WNBA and by 2000 the league had doubled in size. Today there are 13 franchises in the WBNA with talks of future

FUNDAMENTALS OF THE GAME

The original version of basketball was played with nine players. Today, teams can have up to 12 players but only five active players per team are allowed on the court at one time. As a result, there can be up to 7 players sitting on the bench as substitutions or 'subs' for short. Substitutions are unlimited, meaning a team can sub players on and off the court as much as they like. However, subs can only be done once play has stopped and must be approved by the umpires before the substituting player steps onto the court.

Usually leading and guiding the team is a coach, whose role is to give advice, direction and coordinate the offensive and defensive strategies of the team. Other personnel can include an assistant coach, a team manager, statisticians, doctors and trainers who assist the players before, during and after a game.

The length of a basketball game is divided into four 10-minute quarters in international games. The quarters in NBA games are 12-minutes long and in some leagues, such as the NCAA, the games are played not in quarters but over two 20-minute halves. The total length of the four quarters, or two halves, is the actual playing time and the clock is

teams coming from Albuquerque, Atlanta, Atlantic City, the Bay Area, Bentonville (Arkansas), Denver, Kansas City, Knoxville, Memphis, Philadelphia, Pittsburgh, and a possible return to Charlotte.

Rules and Regulations

The rules and regulations of basketball vary among tournaments and organisations worldwide, with elements such as time limits, measurements of the key and the number of personal fouls differing from league to league.

The FIBA rules are generally regarded as the international rules for basketball and are what governs international games and tournaments. However, despite the differing regulations the main object of basketball is the same for all leagues and divisions; to outscore the other team by throwing the ball through the team's designated basket while preventing the opposing team from doing so on their own.

Each basketball game is officiated by a minimum of two umpires or referees who observe and call the game according to the rules and regulations associated with the particular league or competition.

Regulations

FUNDAMENTALS OF THE GAME

stopped every time play is not active. Thus, games generally take much longer to complete than the set allocated time. In addition, players are allowed a 15-minute half-time break and two-minutes are allowed at other breaks, such as quarter times. During the game a team may use a limited number of time-outs, which at the request of the teams coach are stoppages in the game time for a short meeting or huddle with the players. In the case of a tied score at the end of normal time, overtime periods of five minutes are given to continue play and give the teams an extra opportunity to outscore their opponents. At half-time the two teams exchange baskets for the second half so the direction that the teams are shooting is reversed.

To begin every basketball game a jump ball or 'opening tip' is held at the centre of the court, where two opposing players attempt to tap the ball to another member on their team in order to gain possession. In the NBA, a jump ball occurs at the start of the game, the start of any extra period, to settle special situations where penalties cancel out and neither team is previously entitled to the ball and to resolve any held balls. However, in most competitions other than the NBA the alternating possession rule is used to resolve all jump ball situations after the opening tip and is based on the possession arrow on the scorekeeper's table. Whenever such a jump ball situation occurs, the team whose basket that the possession arrow is currently pointing to gets the ball from the nearest sideline rather than holding another jump ball. The arrow then swaps to point to the other team after the ball is thrown in. At the start of the game, the arrow is pointed to the team that lost the opening tip.

Equipment

The beauty with basketball is that it does not require much equipment to play, other than a round object to represent the baskets and of course, a ball. This means the game can be played basically anywhere and at anytime and as a result, basketball has long been regarded as a sport for lower-economic society or urban poor. However, competitive levels do require the use of more equipment including a proper basketball, a basketball court, two basketball rings as well as time clocks, 24-second clocks, scoresheets, scoreboards, alternating possession arrows, umpire whistles and in some leagues, whistle-operated stop-clock technology.

28

FUNDAMENTALS OF THE GAME

In professional or organised basketball the 'court' is the flat, rectangular area that represents the designated surface for play. It has a basket or ring at either end and is free from obstructions. Indoor basketball courts are generally made of hardwood, often maple and are highly polished. Another indoor surface used for basketball courts is plastic interlocking tiles, whilst outdoor courts can be made of asphalt, blacktop or even tarmac. The size of a basketball court can vary from league to league. The regulated court size for international games as set by FIBA, is exactly 91.86ft long × 49.21ft wide (28 × 15 metres), although national federations are allowed to use smaller courts as long as they are at least 26 × 14 metres. The NBA has a slightly bigger court size at 94ft × 50ft (28.65 × 15.24 meters).

In high school and amateur basketball court sizes vary widely often depending on the size of the gymnasium and how much space is available. Different lines, usually painted on to the court surface, signify different areas of a basketball court. The halfway line as the name suggests splits the court into two halves. At the end of each half is the 'key', also known as the 'lane' or the 'paint', which is the area below the basket. Whatever end a team's designated

basket is at is referred to as the frontcourt and is thus the end in which they aim to move the ball towards in order to try and score. At the top of the key is the 'free throw line' and at the bottom is the baseline, which has the ring or basket. The key is 12 feet wide and 15 feet long. The distance from the free throw line to the three-point line is 4 feet 9 inches, whilst the distance from the bottom block to the baseline is 4 feet. The free throw line is where a player awarded to them after being fouled whilst shooting or at least is fouled whilst in the shooting action.

The key is the main area that offensive plays take place and as a result, is also the main area the defence protects, guarding the key in order to protect the offence from getting near the basket. Therefore, the key is considered a restricted area. An offensive player is only allowed to stay inside the key for a maximum of three consecutive seconds when their team is in possession of the ball and themselves outside of the key they must place both feet on the court outside of the restricted area. If an umpire observes an offensive player standing inside the key for longer than the

FUNDAMENTALS OF THE GAME

allocated three seconds, they will blow the whistle, stop play and hand the ball over to the opposing team. There are no restrictions to how long a defensive player stands in the key. Surrounding the key to the baseline on either side is the three-point arc. The distance to the three-point line has changed numerous times in the history of basketball and even today the rules for international, United States amateur and the National Basketball Association each specify different distances. The international distance used in majority of the countries outside of the United States and as set out by FIBA is 20ft 6 inches (6.25m). In the NBA however, the line ranges from 22ft in the corners to 23ft 9 inches at the top of the key.

Early basketball was played with two enclosed peach baskets, one at each end of the court. Physically retrieving the ball from the basket soon proved inconvenient and too time consuming and by 1906 the peach baskets were replaced by metal baskets with holes in the bottom so a long pole could be used to poke the basketball out of the basket rather than having to use a ladder to climb and fetch the ball out of the basket. In 1913, a hoop net was invented so the basketball could fall freely to the ground. This as well as the addition of backboards, which helped keep the ball in court when shots were missed, had a major effect on the development of the game. The games could be played with fewer interruptions and as a result, the overall tempo of a basketball match was increased.

Today, basketball rings are generally made of solid steel and as per the official FIBA rules, must have an inside diameter of a minimum of 450mm and a maximum of 457mm. The rings must also be painted orange and the metal rim can only be a minimum of 16mm and a maximum of 20mm in diameter. The net, made of white cord, has to be suspended from the ring and attached in only 12 places. The net can be no less than 400mm and no more than 450mm in length and must not have any gaps smaller than 8mm. The nets must be manufactured in a way that they check the ball momentarily as it passes through the net, with the upper section of the net semi-rigid to prevent the net from getting tangled up and also to prevent the ball from being trapped or rebounding back out of the net.

The rings must be fixed to the backboard support structure in such a way that any force applied to the ring cannot be transferred to the backboard itself. There must be no direct contact between the ring mounted plate and the backboard diagram. At almost all levels of

FUNDAMENTALS OF THE GAME

competition the top of the basketball ring is exactly 10ft (3.05m) above the court and 4ft (1.2m) from inside the baseline. In junior basketball the height is reduced so that younger players have more of a chance of getting the ball in the ring. The height and placement of the basketball rings are particularly important as the slightest alteration to its position can have an unfavourable effect on a players shooting ability. There are also regulations regarding the rebound or elasticity of the rings, which should be within 35–50 per cent energy absorption range of total impact energy and with a 5 per cent differential between both baskets on the same playing court.

The backboard support structure by which the rings are fixed, can either be secured to the floor, ceiling or wall depending on the league. They are set at least 2,000mm from the outer edge of the end line and must be padded and a bright colour in contrast with the background so it is clearly visible. The actual backboard is either made of glass, fibreglass or wood.

Apart from the court and the basket / rings, the other necessity of basketball is of course the ball. The first game of basketball was played with a soccer ball but as the popularity of the sport grew, so did the need for a specifically made ball. The first purpose-built basketballs were made from patches of leather stitched together with a rubber ball inside. It was only in the late 1950's that Tony Hinkle created a ball that was more visible for both players and spectators and introduced the orange ball that is now in common use. For many years, leather was the material of choice until the late 1990's when use of composite materials gained increased acceptance. Today, there are very rigorous specifications for the balls used in official competition, including the weight, inflation pressure, bounce, circumference, colour and materials used.

According to the FIBA regulations for top-level men's basketball, the spherical ball must be a size 7, which is no less than 749mm and no more than 780mm in circumference and weigh a minimum of 567g and a maximum of 650g. For all women's competitions, the ball must be a size 6, with the circumference between 724mm and 737mm and weighing between 510g and 567g. In either competition, the ball used must state the name of the manufacturer

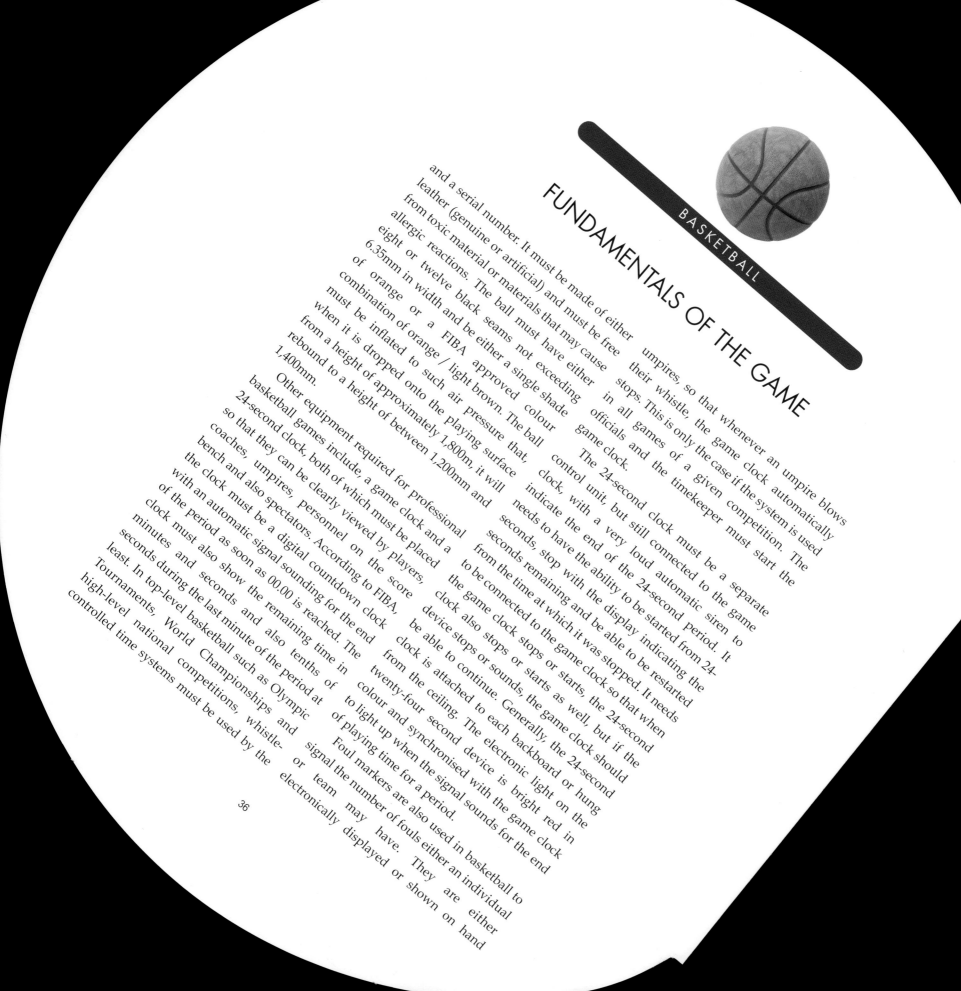

FUNDAMENTALS OF THE GAME

and a serial number. It must be made of either leather (genuine or artificial) and must be free from toxic material or materials that may cause allergic reactions. The ball must have either eight or twelve black seams not exceeding 6.35mm in width and be either a single shade of orange or a FIBA approved colour combination of orange / light brown. The ball must be inflated to such air pressure that, when it is dropped onto the playing surface from a height of approximately 1,800m, it will rebound to a height of between 1,200mm and 1,400mm.

Other equipment required for professional basketball games include, a game clock and a 24-second clock, both of which must be placed so that they can be clearly viewed by players, coaches, umpires, personnel on the score bench and also spectators. According to FIBA, the clock must be a digital countdown clock with an automatic signal sounding for the end of the period as soon as 00.00 is reached. The clock must also show the remaining time in minutes and seconds, and also tenths of seconds during the last minute of the period at least. In top-level basketball such as Olympic Tournaments, World Championships and high-level national competitions, whistle-controlled time systems must be used by the

umpires, so that whenever an umpire blows their whistle, the game clock automatically stops. This is only the case if the system is used in all games of a given competition. The officials and the timekeeper must start the game clock.

The 24-second clock must be a separate clock, with a very loud automatic siren to indicate the end of the 24-second period. It needs to have the ability to be started from 24- seconds remaining and be able to show the seconds, stop with the display indicating the seconds remaining from the time at which it was stopped. It needs to be connected to the game clock so that when the game clock stops or starts as well, the 24-second clock also stops or starts, the game clock so that when device stops or sounds, the game clock should be able to continue. Generally, the 24-second clock is attached to each backboard or hung from the ceiling. The electronic light on the twenty-four second device is bright red in colour and synchronised with the game clock to light up when the signal sounds for the end of playing time for a period.

Foul markers are also used in basketball to signal the number of fouls either an individual or team may have. They are either electronically displayed or shown on hand

FUNDAMENTALS OF THE GAME

paddles that are held up from the score-bench. An alternating possession indicator is also necessary to signal what team is due for possession in cases where the ball can become live with a throw-in rather than a jump ball.

Offence

The role of the offensive team is to attack the basket, aiming to shoot the ball into the basket in order to score the team points without losing or turning over the ball to the defending team. Once a team turns over the ball they become the defending team whilst the team who steals the ball becomes the offensive team. There are various offensive techniques that can be employed in order to attack the basket. A team can only advance the ball towards their basket by either dribbling, passing, rolling or shooting the ball. 'Dribbling' the ball refers to the repetitive action in which a player uses one hand to bounce the basketball continuously and without interruption. It is one of the fundamental skills of playing basketball and is used in order to move the ball up and down the court, use up time, escape from defenders and move closer to the basket or to other

teammates. Only one player can dribble the ball at a time and can be done standing still or on the move.

There are various techniques to dribbling. A crossover dribble is when a player changes their dribbling direction by moving or bouncing the ball from one side of their body to the other. It is generally committed in one quick, swift motion in order to pass the defence by tricking the defender into thinking the ball is going one way and then changing it quickly. As a result, the defender's momentum is usually unable to stay with the player's new dribbling direction. Other flamboyant variations to the traditional crossover is the behind the back or through the leg crossover whereby a player who is dribbling the ball with one hand bounces the ball behind their back or through their legs to the other hand in order to switch the dribbling direction.

A spin move when dribbling is when a player rotates his body in an effort to change the direction they are going. This can be used whilst either dribbling or posting up in the key and is particularly effective as it gets the body in between the ball and the defender in order to prevent him from reaching the ball. However, it has also been met with some

FUNDAMENTALS OF THE GAME

disapproval as the ball handler can become disorientated after performing the act and it also means they are turning their back on the rest of the court and their defender. Hesitation dribbling is committed when a player dribbling the ball intentionally changes pace in order to confuse or falter the defender. Similar to a stutter-step, it makes it more difficult for a defending player to predict the direction and speed of the ball, making it harder to steal the ball.

Whilst dribbling is an offensive action, it also provides an opportunity for the defending team to steal the ball in mid-bounce. There are also other ways a ball can be turned-over to the other team through the act of dribbling. Once a player stops dribbling the ball and holds it, the player must either pass the ball to another player or take a shot. The player cannot start dribbling again once holding the ball and in such cases the game will be stopped for 'double-dribble' and the ball will be given to the opposing team. Similarly, the player cannot take more than two steps with the ball after stopping the dribble or has received the ball and has not yet started dribbling, unless a player is pivoting. Pivoting is when a player who is holding a live ball on the playing court steps once or more in any direction with the same foot while the other foot is kept at its original point of contact with the floor. If a player picks up this pivot foot and takes more than two steps, it is called a travel.

Passing the ball is another fundamental skill of offensive basketball and another way to move the ball up and down the court and to different members of the team either by rolling or throwing the ball. The most basic passing movement is called a chest pass and is performed by pushing the ball outwards from the chest with two hands whilst turning the hands over so the thumbs are pointing down.

A bounce pass is when a player moves the ball to another team member by bouncing the ball off the floor and is one of the hardest for defenders to intercept. Other passes include, an overhead pass, which is used by a football (soccer) throw-in, a jump pass which, is performed whilst the passing player's feet are both off the floor, a blind pass which is when a player looks in one direction but passes the ball to his target in another and a behind the back pass which, as the name suggests, is a pass that is dealt to a target behind the passer's back. No matter what kind of pass a player

FUNDAMENTALS OF THE GAME

undertakes, the ball should always be aimed just in front of the receiver who should have a leading hand extended waiting for the ball.

Another integral part of basketball is shooting. Shooting is the final action a player commits before throwing the ball towards the basket and aiming to get the ball in and through the ring. Two points are rewarded for a shot that is made from anywhere along the baseline, in the key and surrounding area up until the three-point line.

If a shot is made outside the three-point arc, the player and the team is awarded three points. Regardless of where the shot is made from, if the ball goes through the basket and is counted for points, the defensive team gains possession of the ball from underneath the baseline and they automatically become the offensive team, aiming to get the ball down to their front court and score. While there are no restrictions to how a ball is shot through the ring, the proper shooting technique that a player should follow begins with being squared-up or facing the basket, with the feet shoulder-width apart, knees slightly bent and the back straight. The player then holds the ball to rest in their dominant hand's fingertips, slightly above the head and with the other

hand on the side of the ball for guidance. To aim the ball, the player's elbow should be aligned vertically with the forearm facing in the direction of the basket. The ball is shot by extending the shooting arm to become straight. The ball then rolls off the finger tips while the wrist completes a full downward follow-through. The shooting arm should then stationary whilst the ball is released.

There are various methods of shooting. A lay-up shot is when a player either stops dribbling or is passed the ball and then takes two big steps towards the basket and shoots the ball. From this movement, the ball is usually bounced off the backboard and directed into the basket, referred to as a 'bank shot'. The purpose of using the backboard is to try and hit it at an angle so that the speed of the ball is slowed down and the odds of it falling into the ring are increased. A lay-up can also be 'rolled-in' when a player holds the ball with one hand during a lay-up and then lifts his fingers, rolling the ball into the basket. A lay-up that is powerful and quick, with great momentum caused by the player taking a huge step from the forward leap is called a drive.

FUNDAMENTALS OF THE GAME

A regular jump shot is when a player pulls up whilst on their way to the basket and shoots the ball whilst taking both feet off the court and jumping, often giving the shot added height and power. The jump shot is also taken when a player leads towards the key, is passed the ball and then turns and jumps whilst shooting. It can also be taken when a player is dribbling towards the key and then pulls up suddenly and jumps during the shooting action. A turnaround jump shot is when a player posts up, receives the ball facing away from the basket and then has to jump and turn to shoot at the basket turning in the air.

A fade-away shot is a set jump shot, but when the shooter attempts to lean backwards "fading away" from the defender and whilst this type of shot usually has less range than a regular jump shot, it is often harder to defend.

A hook shot is one of the most difficult shots to pull off, but also one of the most effective from inside the key. It is when a player positions themselves in between the ball and the opponent and then releases the ball towards the basket with his outside hand in a "hook" motion. Variations of the hook shot are the jump-hook and the sky-hook, all of which are usually effective because they are very difficult

As well as shooting, there are various offensive plays that teams can do in order to create movement in the key and free up space for easy access to the basket. Offensive plays can be quite complex in professional and top-level leagues. However, the most simple offences are the 'give and go', the 'pick and roll', the 'back door', the 5-out offence as well as basic post plays. The 'give and go' involves a player passing the ball and then running or leading to an open spot and receiving the ball back again for an easy score. 'Pick and roll' is an offensive play in which a player stops to screen or legally block a defender for the player in control of the ball and then slips behind the defender to accept a pass as the handler makes a move towards the basket.

'Back door', is when a player without the ball gets behind the defence and receives a pass for an easy score, usually executed when the defender is unaware of the open space behind them. There are also various offences that involve players, usually two of the five players who are guards or centres, 'posting' or standing just outside the key with their back to the restricted area. From this position they can often be passed the ball and then pivot or take

FUNDAMENTALS OF THE GAME

a drop step into the key for a shot at basket. Often this play is used when the forward players have a height advantage and can get easy access to the ring over their defenders.

A combination of all of these offences can be seen in the 5-out offence, which starts with all five team members out wide from the key. The ball starts with the person at the top of the key, known as the point guard, who then passes it to a team member on either side of the key. The point guard then cuts through the key looking for the pass back before turning and leading to the opposite side to where they passed it. The other members on the opposite side then have to cut into the key and then back out replacing the position of the player to their left. The offence is used by many teams and can be varied to suit different defences and situations. Of course the purpose of offensive plays is to fool the defence and prevent the defence from getting in the way of the offensive motions. Therefore, teams are continuously coming up with new plays and differing techniques in order to trick their opponents.

Violations

Whilst the offensive team has control of the ball there are numerous violations they can commit, resulting in an automatic turnover of the ball to the opposing team. These violations can be categorised into three main areas; floor violations, time violations and goal violations. Firstly, floor violations restrict the way the ball is advanced up or along the court towards a basket. Whilst in possession, the ball must stay within the court. The last team to touch the ball before it goes out of bounds surrenders possession. Apart from travelling or double dribbling, a player's hand cannot be under the ball whilst dribbling, known as 'carrying' the ball. Once a team establishes the ball in the front half of the court, the ball cannot be returned to the backcourt. The ball cannot be kicked or struck with the fist by a member of the offence and if so, the ball is turned over. If committed by a member of the defence, the shot clock is reset and the offensive team is given back the ball.

Time violations involve the limits imposed on the time taken before the ball moves past the halfway line. In international and NBA games teams have eight seconds to move the

FUNDAMENTALS OF THE GAME

ball over the halfway line. In the NCAA and high school games it is 10 seconds. There are also time violations relating to how long a team has to take a shot. In FIBA and NBA regulated games, teams have 24 seconds to attempt a shot. If they do not shoot within that time frame, the game is stopped and the opposing team gets possession. If the team does shoot and the ball hits the ring and is rebounded by an offensive player, the shot clock is reset and they have another 24 seconds to score. This is in addition to the three-second rule which is the time an offensive player can remain in the restricted area of the key as well as the five seconds that a closely guarded player holding the ball has to get rid of the ball by either dribbling, passing or shooting.

Goal violations relate to the shooting of the ball. No player can interfere with the basket or ball while it is on the rim. In international basketball defenders can bat the ball away from the basket once it has touched the rim. If a defensive player does interfere in this manner it is called 'goaltending' and the points, whether the ball goes in or not, are automatically awarded to the shooter. If a teammate of the shooter goal tends the basket

is forfeited and play continues with the defensive team given possession of the ball.

Defence

The aim of the defending team is to win back possession of the ball by stealing, intercepting, rebounding or forcing the opposition team to turn the ball over by committing a violation. The basic defensive stance, regardless of where a player is on the court, is having the feet shoulder width apart with their feet resting on the balls of their feet. Their knees should be bent, their back straight and the buttocks low so that they can no longer see their toes. One hand should be extended out along the side of one knee, while the other hand should be extended out in front of the chest. From this position the defensive player can guide their offence to a direction of their choice or at least, be able to move and follow their player as need be.

The two main defensive techniques are the zone defence and the man-to-man defence, which are often alternated depending on the flow and progress of the game. The zone defence involves players guarding whichever opponent is in their zone. The zone defence

FUNDAMENTALS OF THE GAME

was prohibited in the NBA prior to the 2001 – 2002 season and whilst it is currently allowed, most teams generally do not use this strategy in the NBA. However, it is commonly used in international, college and youth basketball. Most zone defences are signified by a set of numbers that correspond to the number of players on the front of the zone working its way to the back of the zone. For example a 2–3 zone involves two defensive players up the top of the key and three defenders covering areas near the base line and centre of the zone. In the defensive zone, players must keep their hands up and within the passing lanes of the opposition. They need to quickly adjust their positions as the ball and the offensive players move around the key whilst always remaining in between the player in their designated zone and the basket. An important part of the zone defence is communication between the defending players, they need to be very vocal and talk amongst themselves to effectively communicate where they are, where the ball is and where their opponents are or will be. There are many advantages of playing a zone defence. This includes being able to concentrate all the defence around the key and forcing the offensive to stay out wide,

particularly effective if the opponents are poor long-range shooters. Teams who want to slow down the pace of the game and waste time on the clock, often play zone defence as it does not usually involve aggressive pressure on the ball handler. Thus, offensive teams have to pass the ball around the perimeter of the zone, leading to more time being used by the offensive team before committing to a shot.

However, there are also some disadvantages to playing a zone defence. As most of the players are concentrated around the key, the defence tends to be weak on the perimeter and thus, can be ineffective against teams who are good outside shooters. Also, if the defence is not communicating or moving well, gaps can open up that can be exploited by passing or penetrating through the zone. It is also not a good strategy to use if a team is behind in the game, as it gives the offensive team more time to score and thus, less time for the defensive team to catch up. Blocking out an offensive player for rebounds can also be difficult in a zone.

Man-to-Man Defence

Unlike a zone defence, a man-to-man

FUNDAMENTALS OF THE GAME

defence is when each player is assigned to defend and follow the movements of a single player on offence, rather then a designated zone. Often players switch players if needed or leave their players momentarily to double team an offensive player. Up until 2001, man-to-man defence was the only defence allowed in the NBA, which lifted the tempo and energy of the games and created more on-court action for the spectators. While zone defence is now permitted in the NBA, a defender who is standing inside the key is only allowed to play zone defence for three seconds. If the defender violates this rule, a technical foul will be assessed against him and the opposing team is granted one free throw and subsequent possession of the basketball.

The main advantage of a man-to-man defence is that it is more aggressive than the zone defence. It also allows for a team to match up to players who are of the same skill level, size or height. For example, if a there is a really good offensive player on a team, the best defensive player will guard that player. The man-to-man defence can be applied either full court, which is as soon as the offensive team passes the ball in from the base line or after a team turns the ball over or half-court, which is

applied only from the halfway line. The disadvantage of the man-to-man defence is that it often allows the offensive team to run more screens effectively. It also leaves weaker defenders more exposed and open to be exploited by the offence.

Fouls

In basketball, a personal foul is a breach of the rules that concern the illegal personal contact with an opponent. Due to the nature of the game, personal fouls occur on occasions and are not always regarded as unsportsmanlike or illegal. The concept of a foul was set out in the very beginning by Naismith when he defined a foul as running with the ball, holding the ball with the arms or body, striking the ball with the fist or shouldering, holding, pushing, striking or tripping in any way of an opponent. This last definition is the only one that is still applied today. Any number of fouls can be called against a team, irrespective of the penalty. Each foul called must be charged, entered on the score sheet against the individual offender and penalised accordingly.

For contact to be considered a foul against a

FUNDAMENTALS OF THE GAME

player, it must put that player at an advantage over his opponent or in other words, his opponent at a disadvantage. FIBA relies on the cylinder principle to determine whether contact is illegal or not. The cylinder principle is considered as the space within an imaginary cylinder occupied by a player and is limited to the front by the palms of the hands, the rear by the buttocks and the sides by the outside edge of the arms and legs. The arms are not allowed to be any further in front than the position of the feet and should be bent at the elbows so that the forearms and hands are raised.

The cylinder extends from the floor to the ceiling (so the player can jump and remain in his cylinder). A player can occupy any cylinder not already occupied by the opponent. The cylinder a player occupies is protected, that is, no one else is allowed to step or reach into it. If there is a breach of this principle, then there is a possible foul, which the official may or may not penalise after deciding if it placed the opponent at a disadvantage. The NBA does not use the cylinder principle to judge contact but instead rules that a player may not bend or reach in a position that is not normal nor may a player push, hold, kick or purposely trip another player. Elements of time and distance must be regarded when assessing the cylinder principle and relate to the reaction time and distance of another person. For example, a player can not suddenly step or stop in front of a sprinting player even if their cylindrical space was not occupied at the time. The elements of time and distance only apply on players who do not have the ball and thus do not apply to the personal space of the ball carrier.

Charging and Blocking Fouls

A charging foul is illegal contact caused by pushing or moving into another player's torso and can be called on the ball carrier. A blocking foul is illegal contact that hinders the progress of an opponent. Both types of fouls usually involve the player who is dribbling the ball and the player who is guarding the ball carrier. Although an offensive player usually commits a charge and a defensive player usually commits a block, it can sometimes be difficult to determine between a charge and a block and who is at fault. However, it is generally called an offensive charge if the defence was still, moving sideways or backwards (but not forwards) when the contact occurred. This is also applied if the defensive player took a legal guarding position before the contact with both feet on the floor, was hit in the torso and respected the elements of time and distance

FUNDAMENTALS OF THE GAME

and if it is viewed that the offensive player could have stopped or otherwise avoided contact. It is generally called a block if the defensive player was moving forwards or into the offensive player and did not have both feet on the ground.

Other Personal Fouls

Other fouls can be called apart from charging and blocking fouls, including illegal screens, pushing fouls and holding fouls. An illegal screen is when an offensive player attempts to stop a defensive player from guarding another offensive player, but does not respect the elements of time and distance, either initiating the contact, or is moving when the contact occurs. A pushing foul is contact which attempts to displace an opponent by pushing either with the hands or body. A holding foul is called when a player attempts to interfere with another player's freedom of movement by physically restraining the opponent. A player can also be penalised with a foul for 'illegal use of hands,' which is when a player goes outside of his cylinder with his hands and causes illegal contact or 'hand checking,' which is contact by a defensive player against the ball carrier, which impedes a player's speed, rhythm or balance.

The penalties for fouls vary according to the degree, severity and the action the player who is fouled was in when the illegal contact was called. The general penalty for a foul is a single personal foul, which is given to the individual who initiated the illegal contact.

Each player only gets a maximum of five personal fouls, or six in the NBA / WNBA, over the course of a game. If a player uses all five fouls, they 'foul out' and are not allowed to actively participate in the remainder of the game. If a personal foul is not committed against a player who is in the act of shooting, the game shall be resumed with the ball being rewarded to the non-offending team as a throw-in from the nearest sideline or baseline.

Each personal foul is also counted against team. If a team surpasses a preset limit of team fouls in a given quarter, which is a total of four fouls for NBA and international games, the opposing team is awarded free throws on all subsequent fouls for that period.

If a player is fouled whilst shooting, they are also rewarded bonus or free-throw shots, which are taken from the free-throw line after play is stopped and the key is cleared. When

FUNDAMENTALS OF THE GAME

the shooter is fouled inside the three-point line and misses the shot they are awarded two bonus shots. If the shooter is fouled inside the three-point line but makes the shot anyway, they are awarded one bonus shot. Likewise, if a player is fouled outside of the three-point line whilst taking a shot but misses, they are awarded three bonus points and if they are fouled but make the three-point shot, they are awarded one bonus shot.

Other fouls that may attract higher penalties than a standard personal foul or shooting foul include an unsportsmanlike foul, which according to the opinion of the umpire is an illegitimate attempt to directly play the ball that is not within the spirit and intent of the rules. A disqualifying foul is any unsportsmanlike action of a player or member of a team, including substitutes, excluded players, coach, and assistant coach or team supporter. A technical foul is any deliberate or repeated non-cooperation or non-compliance with the spirit of sportsmanship and fair play.

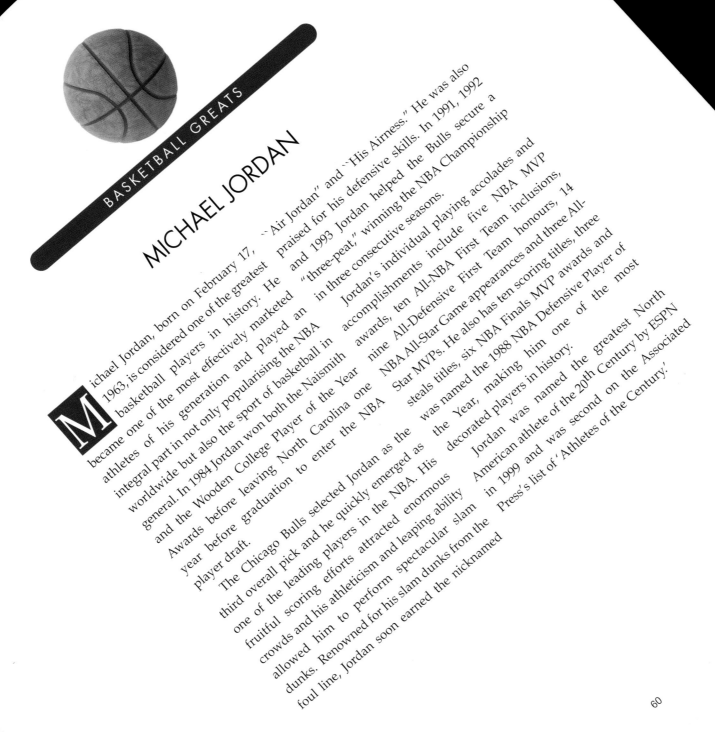

MICHAEL JORDAN

Michael Jordan, born on February 17, 1963, is considered one of the greatest basketball players in history. He became one of the most effectively marketed athletes of his generation and played an integral part in not only popularising the NBA worldwide but also the sport of basketball in general. In 1984 Jordan won both the Naismith and the Wooden College Player of the Year Awards before leaving North Carolina one year before graduation to enter the NBA player draft.

The Chicago Bulls selected Jordan as the third overall pick and he quickly emerged as one of the leading players in the NBA. His fruitful scoring efforts attracted enormous crowds and his athleticism and leaping ability allowed him to perform spectacular slam dunks. Renowned for his slam dunks from the foul line, Jordan soon earned the nickname

"Air Jordan" and "His Airness." He was also praised for his defensive skills. In 1991, 1992 and 1993 Jordan helped the Bulls secure a "three-peat," winning the NBA Championship in three consecutive seasons.

Jordan's individual playing accolades and accomplishments include five NBA MVP awards, ten All-NBA First Team inclusions, nine All-Defensive First Team honours, 14 NBA All-Star Game appearances and three All-Star MVPs. He also has ten scoring titles, three steals titles, six NBA Finals MVP awards and was named the 1988 NBA Defensive Player of the Year, making him one of the most decorated players in history.

Jordan was named the greatest North American athlete of the 20th Century by ESPN in 1999 and was second on the Associated Press's list of 'Athletes of the Century.'

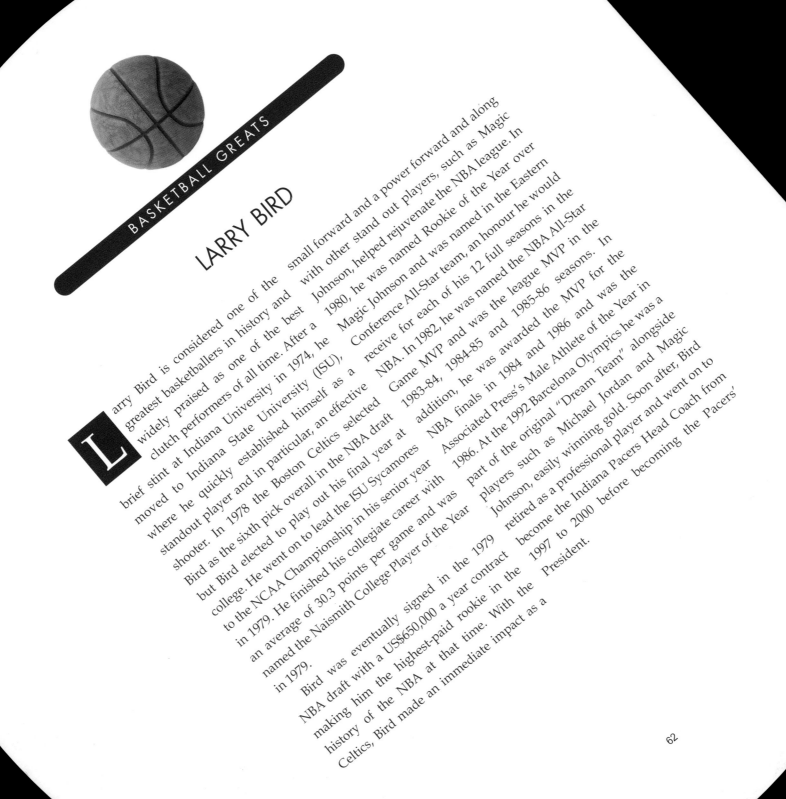

LARRY BIRD

Larry Bird is considered one of the greatest basketballers in history and widely praised as one of the best clutch performers of all time. After a brief stint at Indiana University in 1974, he moved to Indiana State University (ISU), where he quickly established himself as a standout player and in particular, an effective shooter. In 1978 the Boston Celtics selected Bird as the sixth pick overall in the NBA draft but Bird elected to play out his final year at college. He went on to lead the ISU Sycamores to the NCAA Championship in his senior year in 1979. He finished his collegiate career with an average of 30.3 points per game and was named the Naismith College Player of the Year in 1979.

small forward and a power forward and along with other stand out players, such as Magic Johnson, helped rejuvenate the NBA league. In 1980, he was named Rookie of the Year over Magic Johnson and was named in the Eastern Conference All-Star team, an honour he would receive for each of his 12 full seasons in the NBA. In 1982, he was named the NBA All-Star Game MVP and was the league MVP in the 1983-84, 1984-85 and 1985-86 seasons. In addition, he was awarded the MVP for the NBA finals in 1984 and 1986 and was the Associated Press's Male Athlete of the Year in 1986. At the 1992 Barcelona Olympics he was a part of the original "Dream Team" alongside players such as Michael Jordan and Magic Johnson, easily winning gold. Soon after, Bird retired as a professional player and went on to become the Indiana Pacers Head Coach from 1997 to 2000 before becoming the Pacers' President.

Bird was eventually signed in the 1979 NBA draft with a US$650,000 a year contract making him the highest-paid rookie in the history of the NBA at that time. With the Celtics, Bird made an immediate impact as a

LISA LESLIE

Born July 7, 1972, in Gardena, California, Lisa Leslie rose to basketball stardom during her high school years. She was tall for her age and dominated under the basket. She scored a mammoth 101 points in the first half of a high school game and most likely would have broken Cheryl Miller's high school record of 105 points if the opposition team did not forfeit the game at half time. In 1990, she was named the Gatorade Girls Basketball National Player of the Year and went on to be selected in the Pacific Ten Conference first team for the University of Southern California. In 1996, she became one of the original players of the WNBA, playing for the Los Angeles Sparks since the first season in 1997.

In the first two seasons of the WNBA, Leslie led the league in rebounds and throughout the late 1990's, continued to dominate the competition. Leslie led the Sparks to their first WNBA championship in 2001 and became the first player to be named MVP of the league, the All-Star Game and the Finals. On July 30, 2002, Leslie became the first female to score a slam dunk in a WNBA game.In 2006 Leslie collected her 5,000th career point and had an individual career high against the San Antonio Silver Stars with 41 points. She was named the WNBA MVP for the third time that season and to this date, has an unprecented four Olympic Gold medals to her name playing for the USA team in the 1996 Atlanta Olympics, the 2000 Sydney Olympics, the 2004 Athens Games and the 2008 Beijing Olympics.

LAUREN JACKSON

Lauren Jackson started playing basketball at the age of four and quickly developed into an elite player for her high school team. After being invited to play at the Australian Institute of Sport in Canberra as a teenager, Jackson made her debut for the Australian national team, the Opals, in 1997 at just 16-years old. In the Australian women's professional league, the WNBL, she led the Australian Institute of Sport team to a premiership in the 1998-99 season. Soon after she joined the Canberra Capitals and led them to four titles in 1999-2000, 2001-02, 2002-03 and 2005-06 seasons.

In the 2001 WNBA draft, Jackson was an automatic first pick for the Seattle Storm. Standing 196 centimetres tall (6'5") Jackson is effective at both ends of the court. She has a high-shooting percentage combined with determination and mental toughness that makes her a threatening player and is regarded as one of the best players in the history of the WNBA. This was further substantiated when she was voted the WNBA MVP in 2003. The following season she led the Seattle Storm to win the WNBA Championship defeating the Connecticut Suns.

In addition to playing in the WNBA and the Australian national league, Jackson has also played for a Russian club and in 2005, she signed a three-year deal to play for a Seoul based club in South Korea's national league, whilst continuing to play in the WNBA for the Seattle Storm in the Northern Hemisphere summer. In 2007 she was named the MVP for the Korean league.

Jackson also has won three straight silver medals at the 2000, 2004 and 2008 Olympics with the Australian national team. In 2006, she captained Australia to the gold medal over Russia at the World Championship.

KAREEM ABDUL-JABBAR

Kareem bdul-Jabbar played the center position and is regarded as one of the best players of all time. Initially known as Ferdinand Lewis "Lew" Alcindor before converting to Islam and changing his name in 1971, Abdul-Jabbar is the all-time leading NBA scorer with 38,387 points, having collected six NBA titles, six regular season MVP and two Finals MVP awards, fifteen NBA First or Second Teams, a record nineteen NBA All-Star call-ups and averaging 24.6 points, 11.2 rebounds, 3.6 assists and 2.6 blocks per game. He is also the third all-time in registered blocks (3,189), which is even more impressive because this stat had not been recorded until the fourth year of his career (1974).

On offense, Abdul-Jabbar was an unstoppable low-post threat. In contrast to other low-post dominators like Wilt Chamberlain, Artis Gilmore or Shaquille O'Neal, Abdul-Jabbar was a relatively slender player, standing 7'2" but only weighing 225 lbs. However, he made up for his relative lack of bulk by showing textbook finesse and was famous for his ambidextrous skyhook shot, which defenders found impossible to block. It contributed to his high .559 field goal accuracy, making him the eighth most accurate scorer of all time and a feared clutch shooter.

On defence, Abdul-Jabbar maintained a dominant presence. He was selected in the NBA All-Defensive first or second teams eleven times. He frustrated opponents with his superior shot-blocking ability, denying an average 2.6 shots a game.

As a teammate, Abdul-Jabbar exuded natural leadership and was affectionately called "Cap". He was also known for his strict fitness regime, which made him one of the most durable players of all time. In the NBA, his 20 seasons and 1,560 games are performances surpassed only by fellow legend Robert Parish.

Abdul-Jabbar made the NBA's 35th and 50th Anniversary Teams and in 1996, was named one of the 50 Greatest Players of All Time.

SHAQUILLE O'NEAL

Shaquille O'Neal has established himself as a formidable low post presence, with current lifetime averages of 24.7 points on .582 field goal accuracy, 11.2 rebounds and 2.4 blocks per game.

O'Neal's 7 ft 1 in/330-lb (2.16 m / 150 kg) frame gives him a power advantage over most opponents, and for a man of that size, he is quick and explosive. His "drop step", (called the "Black Tornado" by Shaq) in which he posts up a defender, turns around and, using his elbows for leverage, powers past him for a high-percentage alley-oop, has proven an effective offensive weapon. The ability to dunk frequently contributes to his lifetime field goal accuracy of .582, making him one of the most accurate scorers of all time.

O'Neal has been able to step up his performance in big games, having been voted three-times NBA Finals Most Valuable Player. However, because of his poor free-throw shooting, often he is either placed on the bench, or not called upon to take shots, in the closing moments of games, when free throws become important.

As a teammate, he is also noted for his ability to form symbiotic relationships with young, talented guards. Playing alongside O'Neal, talents like Penny Hardaway, Kobe Bryant and Dwyane Wade blossomed into legitimate superstars. Eventually, his relationships with Hardaway and Bryant souredsoured. However, O'Neal embraced his relationship with Wade and the duo won an NBA title in 2006. He was traded from Miami to Phoenix during the 2006-07 season but never brought the Suns the much-desired title. For the 2009 season, O'Neal will be teamed up with LeBron James and the Cleveland Cavaliers.

O'Neal's primary weakness is his free-throw shooting. His lifetime average is 52.8 per cent. He once missed all 11 free throws in a game against the Seattle SuperSonics on December 8, 2000, a record.

LUC LONGLEY

L ucien James 'Luc' Longley was born on January 19, 1969 in Melbourne, Australia. He was the first Australian to play in the NBA. He attended college at the University of New Mexico. Known for his passing ability and free spirit, Longley drew comparisons to fellow redhead Bill Walton upon his entry into the NBA.

Longley was drafted seventh overall by the Minnesota Timberwolves in 1991. After two plus mediocre seasons with the struggling franchise, the 7'2" (218 cm) center was traded to the Chicago Bulls for Stacey King late in the 1993-94 season.

Following the break up of the championship Bulls in 1998, Chicago did a sign and trade with Longley, sending him to the Phoenix Suns for Mark Bryant, Martin Muursepp, Bubba Wells and a conditional first-round draft pick. Longley spent two lackluster seasons with Phoenix, where he gained less attention for his play. He was traded to the New York Knicks prior to the 2000-01 NBA season in what was only the second four-team trade in NBA history. The Suns acquired Chris Dudley as part of the deal together with a first-round draft pick from New York and an undisclosed amount of cash, while New York received Longley, Glen Rice, Travis Knight, Vladimir Stepania, Lazaro Borrell, Vernon Maxwell, two first-round draft picks (from the Los Angeles Lakers and the Seattle SuperSonics) and two second-round draft picks from Seattle. Seattle received Patrick Ewing and the Lakers received Horace Grant, Greg Foster, Chuck Person and Emanual Davis. Longley spent one year with New York before retiring. Longley averaged 7.2 points and 4.9 rebounds per game in his 567 regular season game NBA career. Longley played more NBA games than any other Australian and is widely regarded as one of the best Australian basketballers ever.

Although Longley did not appear in many international matches with the Australian Boomers during his career, this could be due to various injuries that stemmed from an ankle injury that eventually ended his playing days.

Longley attended Scotch College in Perth for the majority of his high schooling, was part-owner of the Perth Wildcats basketball club in the Australian National Basketball League for several years (he played two games for the club in 1986), and is currently the #1 ticket holder of the Fremantle Football Club in the Australian Football League.

YAO MING

Yao was born to his 6'7" (2.01 m) tall father Yao Zhiyuan, and his 6'3" (1.90m) mother Fang Fengdi, who was the captain of the women's national team that won the first Asian Championship in 1976.

He first started playing basketball when he was age nine, and he went to the junior sports school at the same age. When he was examined at age ten he was predicted to grow to the height of 7'3". The Shanghai Sharks invited him to try out for their junior team when he was 13 and he had to practice for 10 hours a day to make the team.

Yao Ming first went overseas to a 1997 Nike camp in Paris, and then went to America the next year to play on an Amateur Athletic Union (AAU) team called High Five.

Yao Ming was initially pressured to enter the NBA draft in 1999 by Li Yaomin, the deputy general manager of the Shanghai Sharks. Li also pressured Yao into signing a contract with Evergreen Sports Inc., which stated that Yao would have to give Evergreen 33 per cent of his earnings. However, Yao quickly terminated the contract after it was determined invalid. Despite the pressure of entering the draft, becoming an NBA player had always been Yao's dream. When Yao Ming decided to enter the 2002 NBA draft, a team of advisors was formed that was collectively dubbed "Team Yao". After Yao's intentions were announced, scouting reports began raving about his shot-blocking, passing, and agility. Some even said that his upside was so tremendous that being selected first overall was virtually guaranteed. Another draft profile called him "the best and most dominant player in China." On draft night, the Rockets picked Yao, who became the first player without any American basketball experience to be selected first overall.

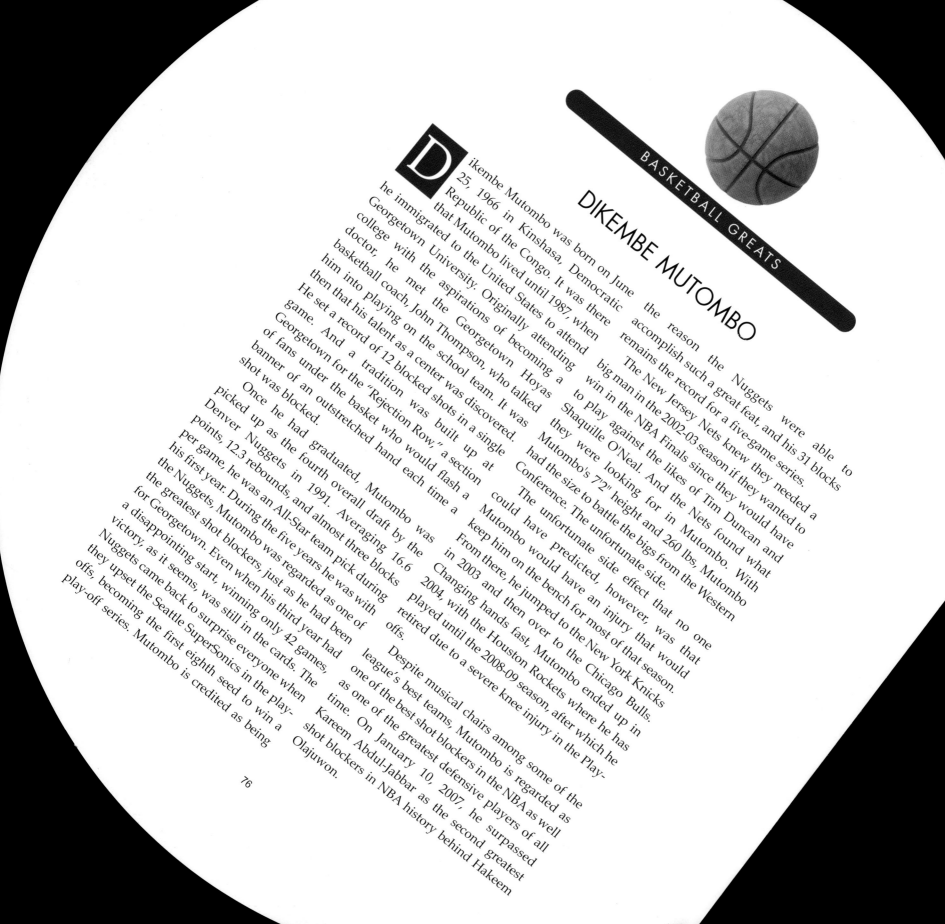

DIKEMBE MUTOMBO

Dikembe Mutombo was born on June 25, 1966 in Kinshasa, Democratic Republic of the Congo. It was there that Mutombo lived until 1987, when he immigrated to the United States to attend Georgetown University. Originally attending college with the aspirations of becoming a doctor, he met the Georgetown basketball coach, John Thompson, who talked him into playing on the school team. It was then that his talent as a center was discovered. He set a record of 12 blocked shots in a single game. And a tradition was built up at Georgetown for the "Rejection Row," a section of fans under the basket who would flash a banner of an outstretched hand each time a shot was blocked.

Once he had graduated, Mutombo was picked up as the fourth overall draft by the Denver Nuggets in 1991. Averaging 16.6 points, 12.3 rebounds, and almost three blocks per game, he was an All-Star team pick during his first year. During the five years he was with the Nuggets, Mutombo was regarded as one of the greatest shot blockers, just as he had been for Georgetown. Even when his third year had a disappointing start, winning only 42 games, victory, as it seems, was still in the cards. The Nuggets came back to surprise everyone when they upset the Seattle SuperSonics in the play-offs, becoming the first eighth seed to win a play-off series. Mutombo is credited as being the reason the Nuggets were able to accomplish such a great feat, and his 31 blocks remains the record for a five-game series.

The New Jersey Nets knew they needed a big man in the NBA Finals since they would have to play against the likes of Tim Duncan and Shaquille O'Neal. And the Nets found what they were looking for in Mutombo. With Mutombo's 7'2" height and 260 lbs, Mutombo had the size to battle the bigs from the Western Conference. The unfortunate side effect that no one could have predicted, however, was that Mutombo would have an injury that would keep him on the bench for most of that season. From there, he jumped to the New York Knicks in 2003 and then over to the Chicago Bulls. Changing hands fast, Mutombo ended up in 2004, with the Houston Rockets where he has played until the 2008-09 season, after which he retired due to a severe knee injury in the Play-offs.

Despite musical chairs among some of the league's best teams, Mutombo is regarded as one of the best shot blockers in the NBA as well as one of the greatest defensive players of all time. On January 10, 2007, he surpassed Kareem Abdul-Jabbar as the second greatest shot blockers in NBA history behind Hakeem Olajuwon.

JORGE GARBAJOSA

Jorge Garbajosa Chaparro, Jr., ("Garbo") was born on December 19, 1977 in Torrejon de Ardoz, Madrid.

At only aged 18, Garbajosa began playing for Tau Vitoria, a Spanish basketball team founded in 1959. He played there for five years, and led the team to victory in the Spanish National Cup during the 1998-1999 season.

From 2000-2004, Garbajosa moved over to the Pallacanestro Treviso, which is more often referred to by its sponsorship name, Benetton Treviso. This basketball club, owned by future Raptors vice-president and assistant general manager, Maurizio Gherardini and Phoenix Suns and New York Knicks head coach, Mike D'Antoni. He averaged 13.8 points, 6.7 rebounds and 2.85 steals per game (a Euroleague best) while in pursuit of the 2002-2003 Euroleague First Team honors. With the Benetton Treviso, Garbajosa also won two national cups, two Super Cups, two Italian championships, and was named the 2003 Eurobasket.com Player of the Year.

Unicaja Málaga, a team based in Málaga, Andalusia and plays in Spain's top league, is where Garbajosa moved next. He spent the seasons from 2004 to 2006 helping them to the

2005-2006 ACB (Asociación de Clubs de Baloncesto: premiere professional basketball league in Spain) league championship and Spanish Cup. In the process, Garbajosa was in the top 15 in scoring and rebounding for 2005-2006 in the Euroleague. He also averaged 13.3 points and 6.4 rebounds outings. Most notable, however, was his ability to shoot 55 per cent from the field and 81 per cent from the free-throw line. During that same year, Garbajosa was honored as the Spanish Cup Finals MVP and All-Euroleague Second Team honors.

In 2006, Garbajosa was signed by the Toronto Raptors to a three-year contract. He was a regular forward starter and played an integral role in getting the Raptors past the .500 mark. He averaged 8.5 points and 4.9 rebounds during that season. If the numbers seem low, it was mainly due to the fact that during a March 2007 game, he was seriously injured, resulting in his inability to play for the rest of the season or the post-season. It seems as though his impact was felt, however, as he received the honor of being named to the NBA All-Rookie Team at the end of that season.

After two seasons in Toronto, Garbajosa returned to Europe for the 2008-09 season to play with Russian team Khimki.

THEODOROS PAPALOUKAS

Born May 8, 1977 in Athens, Greece, Theodoros Papaloukas began his career as a professional basketball player with a small local team in Athens known as the Ethnikos Ellinoroson. He moved rapidly up through the team rank due mainly to his stature (6'7") and ability as a point guard. After Ethnikos Ellinoroson, he played for Ampelokipoi, then Dafni, and ended up with Panionios BC. The latter team is a mid-level traditional in the Greek first league. He astonished most with his agility and outstanding abilities, which then catapulted him to the ranks of member of a major Greek team, Olympiacos. He also became a member of the Greek national team, of which he is still a member.

In June 2002, Papaloukas left Olympiacos to join the well-known and intimidating ranks of the of Russian club CSKA Moscow. Papaloukas made three appearances with the CSKA in the Euroleague Final Fours from the time he joined until 2005. Because of this honor, Papaloukas secured a position among the "who's who" of European basketball at the Eurobasket 2005 in Serbia and Montenegro. He had previously played the championship with CSKA in 2003 in Sweden and once before in 2001 in Turkey when he was still playing with Olympiacos. The CSKA in 2005, however, with Papaloukas' help, experienced a huge win against Russia in the quarterfinals and a win against France in the semifinals, which Greece

came back in a major upset from seven points down with 47 seconds left on the clock. In the finals of that same championship, Papaloukas scored 22 points against Germany, and led the CSKA to its second European title.

Papaloukas also had huge success with the Greek national team, whom he joined in 2000. The biggest highlight came at EuroBasket 2005 in Serbia & Montenegro where he helped Greece to the final in Belgrade. The Greeks knocked off Russia in the quarterfinals before beating France in the semifinals before trailing by seven points with 47 seconds left. And in the 2005 final against Germany, Papaloukas scored 22 points to lead Greece to their second European title.

In 2006, Papaloukas helped CSKA Moscow was their first Euroleague title in 35 years and was named Final Four MVP after scoring 19 points in the semis against Barcelona and 18 points against Maccabi Tel Aviv in the final. That same year, he was also chosen as the best point guard of the Euroleague.

Papaloukas and Greece beat the United States at the 2006 World Championship in the semifinals before losing to Greece in the to take silver. At the club level, Papaloukas and CSKA won the Euroleague title again in 2008. Before the 2008-09 season, he moved back to Greek club Olympiacos and helped them to the Final Four before losing to fellow Greek side Panathinaikos in the semis.

TONY PARKER

William Anthony "Tony" Parker was born on May 17, 1982 in the town of Bruges, Belgium. Raised in France, Parker is the son of Tony Parker Sr., an African-American who played basketball at Loyola University in Chicago. He also played professionally overseas. His mother, a Dutch model, met his father during this stint. As a child, Tony was more interested in soccer than basketball, although he and his brothers enjoyed watching their father play. It was watching Michael Jordan work his magic on the court that won Tony over to the sport for good.

He decided that his position of choice was point guard because he had the speed and agility to make it work.

In 2001, Parker was invited to the summer camp of the San Antonio Spurs. It was in that year that he entered the NBA Draft and was picked up as a point guard as the 28th overall by the Spurs. He played back-up to Antonio Daniels, and made 77 appearances during the regular season of his rookie year. He average 9.2 points, 4.3 assists and 2.6 rebounds in 29.4 minutes per game. On November 30, 2001, Parker became the third French player to play in an NBA game.

Parker has agility, speed and talent. He can hit open jump shots, creating more space for the men of greater stature on his team. And at

the end of his rookie season, he led the Spurs in assists and steals, securing the award of All-Rookie First Team for 2001-2002. This was doubly impressive as Parker was the first foreign-born guard to earn this honor.

The years since have been monumental for Parker. In his second year with the Spurs, he averaged 15.5 points, had 5.3 assists and 2.6 rebounds per game. It was in that year that he also won his first championship ring. He improved even further in the 2004-05 season with 16.6 points, 6.1 assists and 3.7 rebounds per game and ranked 13th in league in assists and third for point guards in field goal percentage. That year, the Spurs won their third NBA championship, the second with Parker on the team.

Parker guided the Spurs to another title – his third – in 2007 as he was named the MVP of the Finals. Parker has also played with the French national team for years, with the biggest highlight coming in 2005 when France won the bronze medal at EuroBasket 2005 in Serbia & Montenegro. With a number of stealthy moves, including leveraging his speed to achieve lay-ups and pick and rolls to outwit his larger opponents, Parker became the first European-born player to be named NBA Finals

MANU GINOBILI

Emanuel David "Manu" Ginobili was born on July 28, 1977 in Bahía Blanca, Argentina. Coming from a family of basketball players, Ginobili's father was a coach at a club in Bahía Blanca where Ginobili learned to play, and his two brothers did (one still does) play, one in the Argentine league and the other in the Spanish Liga Española de Baloncesto.

With his family ties and an ingrained appreciation for the talent of players such as Michael Jordan, Ginobili's love for the game grew until he was able to make his debut in the Argentine league for the Andino Sport Club team of La Rioja from 1995–1996. From there, he was traded to the Estudiantes de Bahía Blanca, a club located in Bahía Blanca, Argentina, where he played until 1998. At that time, the Italian league captured his interest and he moved to Europe to play for the Basket Viola Reggio Calabria team for the 1998-99 and 1999-00 seasons.

It was then that Ginobili entered the 1999 NBA Draft. The San Antonio Spurs picked Ginobili late in the second round as a 57th overall pick. But he didn't sign at that time. Instead, he returned to Italy to play for Kinder Bologna, a team which he helped win the 2001

Italian Championship, the 2001 Euroleague title, as well as the 2001 and 2002 Italian Cups. For his performances, he received the honor of being named MVP of the 2001 Euroleague, Italian league MVP for the 2000-01 and 2001-02 seasons and made the All-Star game roster in the Italian league on three different occasions.

Ginobili participated in the 2002 FIBA World Championship where he helped Argentina place second overall. It was after this series that he joined the Spurs, playing back-up guard for Steve Smith. He had a rough start to that year, but came out shining as the Western Conference Rookie of the Month in March and All-Rookie Second Team at the season's end. That same year, the Spurs challenged the competition in the play-offs, where Ginobili's talents were showcased. He was played in every game as he took opponents by surprise with his impressive scoring ability. The Spurs won their second ever championship that year, and Ginobili was elected as Argentina's top sportsman by the country's main newspaper publication.

Over the 2003-04 season, Ginobili started half of the 77 games in the regular season and averaged an impressive 12.8 points, 4.5 rebounds, 3.8 assists, and 1.8 steals per game.

MANU GINOBILI

That year, the Spurs went into the play-offs where Ginobili's stats rose to 13 points, 5.3 rebounds and 3.1 assists per game. Following the NBA season, Ginobili joined the Argentina national team at the 2004 Olympics in Athens. On opening day, Ginobili scored a "buzzer beater" with .7 seconds on the clock to win against Serbia and Montenegro. Argentina was the first team other than the U.S. to win the gold medal in 16 years. Ginobili was named MVP with 19.3 points and 3.3 assists per game.

Ginobili debuted in the elite mid-season showcase during the 2004-05 season as a reserve in

the 2005 Western Conference All-Star team. Scoring all time career highs with 20.8 points and 5.8 rebounds per game, Ginobili made plays that were integral in capturing San Antonio's third ever championship. At the end of the series, he was the second leading team scorer. Season 2005-06 was filled with injury for Ginobili, but he returned again full strength for the 2006-07 season. It was then that he produced statistics that were closely aligned with those of the 2004-05 year, and helped lead the Spurs to their fourth overall championship victory.

HAKEEM OLAJUWON

Born on January 21, 1963, into a middle-class, Yoruba (an ethno-linguistic African group) family in Nigeria, Hakeem Abdul Olajuwon was the third of six children. Playing soccer as a youngster, Olajuwon learned clever footwork techniques and agility that would later assist him in his professional basketball career, namely his shot-blocking talent. It wasn't until the age of 15, however, that Olajuwon took up basketball when he entered a local tournament. From that day forward, he was hooked.

Olajuwon emigrated from Nigeria to play basketball for the University of Houston. As opposed to being merely asked to come and visit the university and meet with the coaching staff in 1980. It was

at that time that he and his teammates formed a "fraternity" or so they called it, aptly named "Phi Slama Jama" for the team's ability to frequently slam dunk the basketball.

After being redshirted in his freshman year, Olajuwon was advised to team up with NBA MVP winner Moses Malone, who could serve as a mentor to Olajuwon. He participated in workouts and one-on-one games with Malone throughout the summer before his sophomore year. He came back to school a changed man, playing better than ever before and helped take his team to two consecutive years of NCAA championship games. Olajuwon won the 1983 NCAA Tournament Player of the Year award, the last player in history from a losing team in the final game to be honored as such.

In 1984, the NBA Draft Lottery was not in practice (1985), so Olajuwon took a chance and

HAKEEM OLAJUWON

left college ball betting that the Houston Rockets would win the coin toss and get the number one draft choice. They did, and as the top amateur prospect, Olajuwon was picked to join the Houston Rockets over other well-known collegians as Michael Jordan and Charles Barkley. The Rockets improved immensely with Olajuwon's help, going from 29-53 in the 1983-84 season to 48-34 in 1984-85. Joining with fellow teammate, Ralph Sampson, the duo formed the original "Twin Towers" of basketball. Olajuwon also perfected a set of fakes and spins that became his trademark—the Dream Shake. He was known as having the best footwork for a man of his size. He averaged 23.5 points, 11.5 rebounds and 3.4 blocks per game in the 1985-86 season.

Olajuwon continued making impressions on the court, such as in the 1988-89 season, where he finished as the league leader in rebounds (13.5) and in the 1989-90 season when he out-rebounded even David Robinson with an average of 14 per game, giving him the NBA rebounding crown. And in that season, he also set the record for most blocked shots, and has yet to be out-blocked on game average

as of 2007. He played successfully for the Rockets until 2001, when he was traded to the Toronto Raptors, where he retired in 2002 as the all-time league leader in total shots blocked at 3,830. His #34 jersey was retired in his honor.

Other major accomplishments included:

2x NBA champion (1994, '95)
2x NBA Finals MVP (1994, '95)
1x NBA MVP (1994)
2x Defensive Player of Year (1993, '94)
6x All-NBA First Team (1987, '88, '89, '93, '94, '97)
3x All-NBA Second Team ('86, '90, '96)
3x All-NBA Third Team (1991, '95, '99)
5x All-Defensive First Team ('87, '88, '90, '93, '94)
12x All-Star
Olympic gold medalist (1996)

He is one of the only four players in NBA history to record a quadruple-double

He is the only player in NBA history to place in the top ten for blocks, scoring, rebounding, and steals.

Olajuwon ranks 7th all-time in steals and is by far the highest ranked center.

STEVE NASH

Steve Nash was born in Johannesburg, South Africa on February 7, 1974. At the age of only 18 months, however, his parents moved the family to British Columbia, where they settled. Nash and his younger brother both played soccer and ice hockey, and Steve did not actually get into basketball until somewhere between the ages of 12 and 13. Soon after, he told his mother that he was going to play in the NBA and become a star. How prophetic that statement was.

For whatever reasons, Nash was overlooked by scouts from major universities, until the head coach from Santa Clara University in California went on a tip to see Nash play. He was the only American scout in the stands and offered Nash a scholarship for the 1992-93 season. For the first time in five years, Nash led the Santa Clara Broncos to a West Coast Conference (WCC) title and a huge upset win over the No. 2 seeded team Arizona in the NCAA end of the collegiate season tournament. Nash hit six straight free throws in the last 30 seconds of the game. In the 1994-95 year, Nash was named Conference Player of the Year. Nash was the league leader in scoring and assists. It was in the following year that Nash saw his efforts come to fruition with

attention from the national media and scouts. He also won Conference Player of the Year for the second consecutive time, making him the first Santa Clara player to do so since Kurt Rambis. He completed his college career as the all-time leader in assists (510), three pointers (made and attempted, 263-656) and free throw percentage (862) at Santa Clara. His jersey was retired in 2006 in his honor.

In the 1996 NBA Draft, Nash was selected as 15th overall by the Phoenix Suns. While improving and proving his worth over time, his stint in Phoenix did not last long and he was traded to the Dallas Mavericks in 1998. There, Nash proved his worth as one of the best point guards in the NBA. His first year, Nash started 40 games and averaged 7.9 points, 2.9 rebounds and 5.5 assists per game. By 2000-01, however, Nash was averaging 15.6 points and 7.3 assists per game. With a powerhouse team leading the way, consisting of Nash, Dirk Nowitzki, Michael Finley and Josh Howard, the Mavericks went to the play-offs for the first time in more than a decade. In 2004 Nash returned to the Phoenix Suns and had loads of success during the regular season, winning the 2005 and 2006 MVP awards. But Nash's teams could never go deep into the

BORIS DIAW

Boris Babacar Diaw-Riffiod, better known as Boris Diaw, was born on April 16, 1982 in Cormeilles, France. At the age of only 21, Diaw was drafted by the Atlanta Hawks in the first round, twenty-first overall in the 2003 NBA Draft. In his first year, he did well, averaging 4.5 points, 4.5 rebounds, 2.4 assists per game and shot 44.7per cent from the field. He was known for playing solid defense. But his career with the Hawks was to be short-lived. Diaw was traded to the Phoenix Suns just after his second year.

It is because of his performance with the Suns and the way he developed over the first several seasons that Diaw has earned the reputation as one of basketball's best. He showed that he was versatile in that he could play any position from point guard to center. He also earned the nickname "3D".

In the 2005-06 season, his game had improved so much, he was averaging 13.3 points, 6.9 rebounds, 6.2 assists and 1.05 blocks per game. He also achieved .526 field goal percentage and 73.1per cent from the free-throw line. This performance garnered him the Most Improved Player with 80 votes. He was also crowned Most Improved with 80 first-place votes by sports writers and broadcasters and a total of 489 overall votes.

18.7 points, 6.7 rebounds, 5.2 assists, and 1.1 blocks per game in the 2006 NBA play-offs. His free-throw line percentage also increased to 76per cent in three play-off rounds. His career high came in the 2006 Western Conference Finals against the Dallas Mavericks when he scored a total of 34 points, including a 7-foot turnaround jumper with 0.5 seconds in regulation, which won the game for Phoenix.

What Diaw has become probably best-known for is his talent for the triple-double. He achieved his first on January 31, 2006 while playing Philadelphia. He had scored 14 points, 13 assists, 11 rebounds, one block and no turnovers in 39 minutes, making him the first French NBA player to attain such a feat. His second came just a little over one month later in a game against the Mavericks. And yet again, he found a third triple-double one month after that in a game against the Golden State Warriors. For his third, he scored 11 points, 11 rebounds, 16 assists, three blocks, and 2 steals, all in just 42 minutes.

In July 2006, Diaw was chosen as the captain of the French national Team, which he led in the 2006 FIBA World Championship with 107 points and 22 assists in 9 games. He also helped France qualify for EuroBasket 2009 and then the 2010 World Championship in Turkey.

HIDAYET TURKOGLU

Born March 19, 1979 of Bosnian descent, but was born and lived his early life in Istanbul, Turkey. At 6'10", Turkoglu is a solid shooter from both inside and outside the three point line, is a good rebounder and good passer. He plays the position of small forward but due to his size and combination of abilities he offers on the court means that he is highly versatile, and has also been able to play four positions, ranging from point guard to power forward. He is considered to be the best all-round player that Turkey has ever produced.

In 1996, Turkoglu joined Efes Pilsen, a club within the Turkish basketball league that happens to be the most successful basketball club in Turkey's history. He played with the club from 1996-2000, when he was selected as the 16th pick by the Sacramento Kings in the first round of the 2000 NBA Draft - becoming the first Turkish-born player in the NBA. In his second year with the Kings, he was a finalist for the NBA's Sixth Man of the Year Award based on his average of 10.1 points, 4.5 rebounds, and two assists per game - and all that was just off the bench.

In 2003, Turkoglu was traded to the San Antonio Spurs. In the one year he played for them, Turkoglu averaged 9.2 points, 1.9 assists, 4.5 rebounds and one steal per game. He became a free agent, however, in 2004 and that sent him onto the Orlando Magic. For the 2004-05 season, Turkoglu averaged 14 points, 2.3 assists, and 3.5 rebounds in the 2004-05 season. He then raised the bar in the 2005-06 season with averages of 14.9 points, 2.8 assists, and 4.3 rebounds. While time may dwindle ability and agility on the court for other basketball players, Turkoglu excelled during the 2007-08 season, posting career highs in points (19.5), rebounds (5.7) and assists (5.0). The following season he helped the Magic to the NBA Finals before losing to the L.A. Lakers. After the season he was signed and traded to the Toronto Raptors.

Turkoglu has also played for the Turkish national team, guiding them to the silver medal at EuroBasket 2001. He will be leading figure for Turkey at the 2010 World Championship in Turkey.

PREDRAG STOJAKOVIC

Predrag "Peja" Stojakovic was born on June 9, 1977 in Slavonska Pozega, SR Croatia, Yugoslavia. Born to Serbian parents, Stojakovic grew up in Belgrade after he and his family fled during the Yugoslav wars. From there, at the age of 16, Stojakovic moved onto Greece where he would be better enabled to play professional basketball. He signed with PAOK BC of the Greek league based in Thessaloniki, where he played for four seasons. During his tenure, he scored a well-remembered three-pointer in a game against Olympiacos in the Greek play-offs. And in his final season, Stojakovic was awarded Most Valuable Player for the league with 23.9 points, 4.9 rebounds, 2.5 assists and 1.2 steals.

During the 1996 NBA Draft, Stojakovic was picked in the first round as 14th overall pick by the Sacramento Kings while still playing for Greece. He continued to play for Greece until he was signed with the Kings for the 1998-99 season. He sat on the bench for the two seasons that followed, but a breakthrough was on the horizon. During the 2000-01 season, Stojakovic averaged 20.4 points, 5.8 rebounds and made 40 percent of his shots from three-point range. That season he finished second in the voting for the Most Improved Player award. During the 2001-02 season he made the NBA All-Star Game and his season scoring improved to 21.2 points per game, a career high in shooting of .484 and a three-point percentage of .416. For that year as well Stojakovic won the three-point shooting during the All-Star Weekend.

PREDRAG STOJAKOVIC

Selected again as an All-Star in 2003-04, Stojakovic was second in the league with scoring (24.2 ppg) and finished fourth in MVP voting. This secured him a spot on the All-NBA Second Team. Despite missing 16 games to an injury, Stojakovic still averaged 20.1 points per game in the 2004-05 season as well.

Moving around for the next couple of seasons, Stojakovic was traded to the Indiana Pacers on January 25, 2006. He re-signed with the Pacers for the 2006-07 season but was dealt to the New Orleans/Oklahoma City Hornets. In his eighth game with the team, Stojakovic scored a career high 42 points. Unfortunately, due to a number of injuries, Stojakovic played just 13 games during the 2006-07 season. But it seems as though all might be well with the player deemed "one of the best to come out of

"Serbia" as he returned to the game for the 2007-08 season and led the Hornets deep into the play-offs. New Orleans returned to the play-offs in 2008-09 as well with Stojakovic playing a major role.

Stojakovic also enjoyed plenty of success with the Yugoslavia national team. The team captured the bronze medal at EuroBasket 1999 and then won the gold medal at the 2001 European Championship during which Stojakovic won the MVP award. The sharp-shooter helped Yugoslavia to the gold medal one year later at the 2002 World Championship, where he was named in the All-Tournament Team along with fellow NBA stars Manu Ginobili, Dirk Nowitzki and Yao Ming.

CHARLES BARKLEY

Charles Wade Barkley was born on February 20, 1963 in rural Leeds, Alabama, which is just outside of Birmingham. Barkley attended school in Leeds and high school there as well, where, as a junior was only 5'10" tall. However, that following summer, he bloomed to 6'4", earning him a starting position on the school basketball team as a senior. He averaged 19.1 points, 17.9 rebounds and the team had a 26-3 record on their way to the state semi-finals. It wasn't until the state semifinals, however, that Barkley got some much-deserved attention from college scouts when he scored 26 points against Alabama.

Barkley played the center position for Auburn University where he led the team in rebounds for each of the three years he played. Despite being somewhat overweight on a frame that wasn't as tall or broad as most with his same weight, Barkley performed on the court with the agility of a much smaller player, considered as the crowd pleaser of most games with a number of dunks, blocked shots, and dribbling that lasted the length of the court. It was due to his stature and his talent he earned the nickname "The Round Mound of Rebound." He averaged 14.1 points on 65.2 percent filed goal shooting, 9.6 rebounds, 1.6 assists, and 1.7 blocks per game, and earned honours including Southeastern Conference Player of the Year for 1984, two All-SEC selections (1983-1984), two Second Team All-SEC (1982-83), one Third Team All-American selection (1984), and SEC Player of the Decade for the 1980s by the Birmingham Post-Herald.

In the 1986 Draft, Barkley was the fifth pick in the first round by the Philadelphia 76ers. During the regular season, Barkley averaged 14 points and 8.6 rebounds per game and earned a spot on the All-Rookie team during his first year. In his second year, he averaged 20 points with 12.8 rebounds per game and became the 76ers power forward, in which he helped the team make it to the play-offs where he averaged 25 points, 57.8 per cent shooting from the field and 15.8 rebounds.

It was following the retirement announcement of Julius Erving in the 1987-88 season that Barkely stepped up to fill his shoes as the 76ers franchise player. He played 80 games (more than 300 minutes) and averaged 28.3 points on a 58.7 per cent field goal shooting and 11.9 rebounds per game. The last

CHARLES BARKLEY

season that Barkley played with the 76ers was the 1991-92 season, in which he scored 23.1 points on 55.2 per cent shooting and 11.1 rebounds per game. He earned his sixth straight All-Star appearance and was named in the All-NBA Second Team, making it his seventh straight appearance on either a first or second team. When he left the 76ers that year to play for the Phoenix Suns, he was fourth in the team's history in total points with 14,184, third in scoring with 23.3 points per game, and placed in the top ten in three other categories.

In the 1992-93 season with the Suns, Barkley averaged 25.6 points on 52 per cent shooting, 12.2 rebounds and 5.1 assists per game. He also won the league's

MVP award and made his seventh consecutive All-Star appearance. Barkley played with the Suns through the 1995-96 season, in which he led the team in scoring, rebounds, and steals. He also achieved a career-high that season with 77.7 per cent free throw shooting and posted his 18th career triple-double. In that same year, he also became one of only ten players to score 20,000 points and 10,000 rebounds. Barkley would go onto play with the Houston Rockets before retiring, where he

would achieve another major record becoming the second player in NBA history to accumulate 23,000 points, 12,000 rebounds and 4,000 assists in his career.

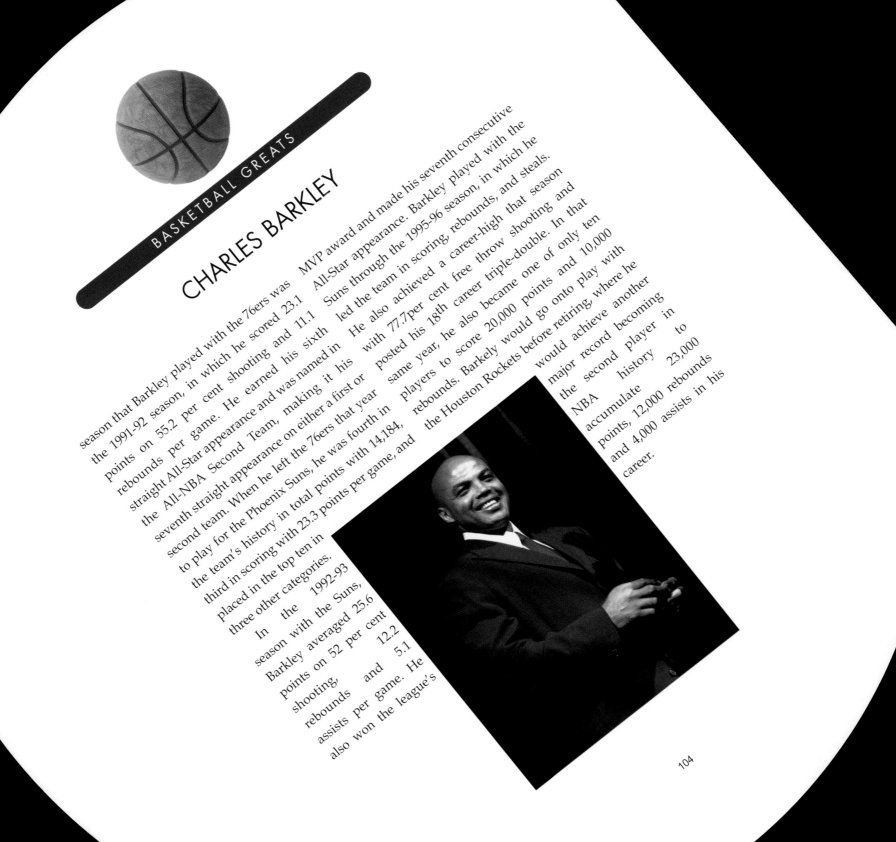

MAGIC JOHNSON

E arvin Effay Johnson, Jr. was born on August 14, 1959 in Lansing Michigan. He grew up loving basketball and played for Lansing High School at just the age of 15. In his sophomore year, Magic Johnson had a game with a triple-double 36 points, 16 rebounds and 16 assists. It was after that game that a reporter deemed him "Magic" Johnson. Johnson attended Michigan State University for college where he planned to focus on a career in communications (he wanted to be a commentator). However, as point guard Johnson led the Michigan team, averaging 17 points, 7.9 rebounds, and 7.4

assists as a freshman. His team made it to the NCAA Championship game that same year where Johnson played against Larry Bird (Indiana State University) and won 75-64.

Johnson was recognized as Most Outstanding Player for the Final Four. He completed his college career with 1,059 points, 471 rebounds and 348 field goals out of 752.

Having excelled rapidly playing college ball, Johnson decided to leave college early and make himself eligible for the 1979 NBA Draft. He was the Los Angeles Lakers' first overall pick. In his rookie season (1979-80), Johnson added a new style of play to the game, one that was known as up-tempo or energetic. He provided the team and the crowd with a great mix of winning techniques such as spinning feeds, overhand bullets under the basket, no-look passes off the fastbreak, and pinpoint alley-oops. It was this new style of basketball that became known as "showtime."

In that same, rookie year, Johnson average 18 points, 7.7 rebounds, 7.3 assists per game,

MAGIC JOHNSON

and led the league in triple-doubles with a rate of 10 points, 10 rebounds, and 10 assists per game. During the 1981-82 season, the owner of the Lakers, Jerry Bus, was such a fan of Johnson, that when the head coach and Johnson could not see eye to eye, it was the coach that was sent packing. And when the new coach, Pat Riley joined the team, Johnson went on to perform a very strong season with 18.6 points, 9.6 rebounds, 9.5 assists, and 2.7 steals per game. Those statistics earned him a position on the All-NBA Second Team. Johnson became one of only three players in the NBA who at that time had scored at least 700 points, 700 rebounds and 700 assists in the same season.

In the regular 1984-85 season, Johnson averaged 18.3 points, 6.2 rebounds and 12.6 assists per game. He followed that performance with another great season the following year, averaging 18.8 points, 5.9

rebounds, and 12.6 assists. And then came the 1986-87 season, in which Johnson performed at his best. He averaged 23.9 points, 6.3 rebounds and 12.2 assists, earning him the first MVP award of his career. In the 1988-89 season as well, Johnson earned an MVP for his 22.5 point, 7.9 rebound and 12.8 assist average. He followed that up with yet another MVP earning the following season.

Johnson played for the Lakers until announcing that he had been diagnosed with HIV. He took leave on his own, although still being paid by the franchise. Despite his diagnosis, Johnson still was chosen for the 1992 US Olympic baseketball team, aptly named the "Dream Team." Johnson would make an attempted return to basketball for the 1992-93 season, but only played for the pre-season and then announced his retirement. He is still known as one of the top ten best players in the league's history.

108

JULIUS ERVING

J ulius Winfield Erving II was born on February 22, 1950 and was raised in Roosevelt, New York. He played basketball in high school where he earned his nickname "Doctor J" for his own method of playing or technique. After high school, he went onto the University of Michigan where he played two varsity seasons and averaged 26.3 points and 20.2 rebounds per game. For that, he was one of only five players in NCAA Men's Basketball to average more than 20 points and 20 rebounds per game. At the time when Erving left college basketball, the professional league(s) was in a state of limbo being split between two leagues. Erving joined the American Basketball Association (ABA) with the Squires as a free agent in 1971.

He was a powerhouse when it came to dunking, scoring 27.3 points per game as a rookie and was chosen for the All-ABA Second Team as well as the ABA All-Rookie Team. At first chance when he was eligible, Erving was picked up by the Milwaukee Bucks as 12th overall in the first round. He then moved on to join the Atlanta Hawks right before the 1972-73 season, where he played three exhibition games. However, Erving received a legal injunction that forced him back to the ABA Squires, where he achieved a career-best

average of 31.9 points per game. Erving was traded to the New York Nets in 1973 and led the team to its first ABA title during the 1973-74 season. He was a crowd pleaser and a game winner, and that helped in legitimizing the ABA's existence. Despite these effots, the ABA was failing and by 1976, the Nets applied for admission to the NBA. They were denied and had to continue playing for one more year in the defunct league, which proved not to hinder Erving's performance who averaged 34.7 points per game and earned the title of Most Valuable Player in the play-offs.

In 1980, Erving became known for his legendary baseline move, his behind-the-board reverse layup, which he first displayed in a game against Kareem Abdul-Jabaar. Erving continued to play for the 76ers until his retirement after the 1986 season. It was for those last few games that he played, that fans flocked to see him play, selling out every single game. At retirement, he had played 836 games. And, in his combined career between the ABA and NBA, he had scored more than 30,000 points. He is one of only a few to have his number retired by two teams, the Nets (#32) and the 76ers

PATRICK EWING

Born on August 5, 1962, Patrick Aloyius Ewing lived in Kingston, Jaimaica until the age of 13 when he came to the United States with his family. Settling in Cambridge, Massachusetts, Ewing learned to play basketball at Cambridge Rindge and Latin, a public high school. From there, he went onto Georgetown University where he received a scholarship for the 1981-82 season, his freshman year. He was one of the first freshman to start and star on the varsity team. In his senior year, Ewing was ranked number one in the nation and was easily one of the best college basketball players of his era, playing in three NCA tournaments out of his four years and making the first-team All-American in 1983, 1984 and 1985.

The New York Knicks won the Draft Lottery of 1985 and picked Ewing as their first overall. He earned the title of Rookie of the Year with 20 points, 9 rebounds, and two blocks per game. With the Knicks, he was a NBA All-Star 11 times, a one-time member of the All-NBA First team, a member of the All-NBA Second team six times, and the NBA All-Defensive Second team three times. He was also a member of the 1992 Olympic Dream Team, winning a second gold medal and was

named one of the NBA's 50 greatest players in 1996.

In the 1993-94 season, Ewing and the Knicks made a run for the finals for the first time since 1973. While the Knicks were unable to win the series, Ewing made the most of his time in play-offs, setting a record for the most blocked shots in a finals game series. The Knicks made yet another trip to the finals the following year with Ewing's help, but were defeated again. In his final season with the Knicks in 1999-00, Ewing and his team took one last trip to the finals but again found the title to be elusive. Ewing left the Knicks at the end of that season to join the Seattle SuperSonics. He played there for one season and then played for the Orlando Magic the season following that. He then announced his retirement on September 18, 2002.

Considered one of the greatest players not only for the Knicks but also for the entire NBA, Ewing had become the 10th player in the history of the NBA to record 22,000 points and 10,000 rebounds in 1999. He had also been in the top ten in several categories, including: field goal percentage (eight different times), rebounds, and total rebounds (eight times), points and blocks per game for 13 years.

WILT CHAMBERLAIN

Wilton Norman "Wilt" Chamberlain was born on August 21, 1936 in Philadelphia, Pennsylvania to a family with a total of nine children.

Having a great amount of both speed and agility, Chamberlain had an affinity for track and field. He could jump 6'6" and run 440 yards in 49 seconds. He could also clear 22 feet in the long jump. Fortunately, Chamberlain discovered basketball in the seventh grade and at 6'11", easily made it into the team at Philadelphia's Overbrook High School during his freshman year. He immediately found a name for himself on the court, becoming one of the most powerful high school players of all time, with a grand total of 2,252 points for his high school career. His nickname, "The Big Dipper," was born from his ability to intimidate on the court due to his overbearing stature and natural-born talent. Although many universities were interested in recruiting Chamberlain, he decided to play for the University of Kansas.

Chamberlain played for the Kansas Jayhawks freshman team since freshmen were not allowed to play on varsity. In his very first game, Chamberlain dominated the court, scoring a total of 52 points, 29 rebounds and four blocks. He also continued to improve his basketball. And, in his debut on the varsity team, all his training paid off, making the All-American squad and leading the Jayhawks to the NCAA finals. Chamberlain was elected the Most Outstanding Player in the Final Four. For his two seasons with Kansas, Chamberlain averaged 29.9 points and 877 rebounds. His college performance garnered him media coverage worldwide. Until he was eligible to play in the NBA, Chamberlain next decided that he would pass the time with the Harlem Globetrotters.

When eligible, Chamberlain was drafted by the Philadelphia Warriors, bringing him back to his home. In his rookie season, he averaged 37.6 points and 27 rebounds. He also own the NBA MVP, Rookie of the Year, and NBA All-Star Game MVP awards. After a threat of retirement, Chamberlain stayed onto blow away his own performance from the previous year with 38.4 points and 27.2 rebounds per game. He also became the first player to break the 3,000-point mark and became the only (and still the only) to break 2,000 rebounds in a single season.

WILT CHAMBERLAIN

Chamberlain continued to play for the Warriors until 1965 when he was traded to the 76ers, where he posted 34.7 points and 22.9 rebounds on average during his first season. He played for the 76ers until 1968 when he was again traded to the Los Angeles Lakers. The team blew through the play-offs with Chamberlain scoring 20.5 points and 21.1 rebounds on average per game. He injured his knee during his second season and was only able to play a total of 12 games, but came back the following season with the help of Gail "Stumpy" Goodrich to

score an average of 20.7 points, 18.2 rebounds and 4.3 assists per game.

Chamberlain's last season came in 1972-73, in which he scored an average of 13.2 points and 18.6 rebounds. This won him the rebounding crown for the 11th time in his career and an all-time shooting record from the field of .727 (the ninth time he led the league in field goal percentage).

Chamberlain was inducted into the Basketball Hall of Fame in 1978 and named one of basketball's 50 greatest players in 1996.

JOHN STOCKTON

John Houston Stockton was born on March 26, 1962 in Spokane, Washington. He lived there with his family straight on through college, where he attended the local, Gonzaga University. He played basketball for Gonzaga beginning in the 1980-81 season as a point guard where he averaged 20.9 points per game with 57 per cent from the field in his senior year.

Stockton was drafted by the Utah Jazz in the first round of the 1984 NBA Draft. As a point guard, he average a career double-double, with 13.1 points and 10.5 assists per game. He was considered one of the toughest players in the league, having been tagged as "old school" due to his preference toward rough housing and physical prowess on the court. Stockton was usually paired in the headlines with teammate Karl "the mailman" Malone, with whom he played with in a record 1,412 games. It was Stockton's keen ability to always find the "open man," who more often than not was Malone, which made the duo so powerful.

In his career, Stockton recorded 15,806 assists, which at the time was 5,000 more than his nearest competitor. Stockton to this day holds five of the top six single-season assist totals and is one of only three players in the

NBA to record more than 1,000 assists in a single season, which he did seven times. He also had the most steals with 3,265. To date, there are only four players who have achieved more than half of Stockton's steal total. To further add to his portfolio of talent and records, Stockton also shot over 50 per cent from the floor over the duration of his career.

With the Jazz, Stockton made it to the NBA play-offs in every single one of his seasons. He appeared in 10 All-Star games and was awarded the title of co-MVP in 1993 second only to Karl Malone. He was selected as the All-NBA First Team twice, All-NBA Second Team five times, NBA All-Defensive Second Team six times, and the All-NBA Third Team three times. In addition to appearing on the Dream Team in the 1992 and 1996 Olympics, Stockton was also named one of the greatest 50 NBA players of all time.

Having played with the Jazz for a total of 19 seasons, Stockton has the second longest tenure with a single team in the NBA's history. He missed only 22 games, 18 of which were in a single season. Stockton is ranked among those players such as Carl Malone, Charles Barkley and Reggie Miller who are considered the greats of basketball despite never winning a championship.

118

ISIAH THOMAS

I siah Lord Thomas III was born April 30, 1961 in Chicago, Illinois. He spent his childhood living in a poverty-stricken neighborhood, playing on the local outdoor courts with his brother and friends. Thomas attended St. Joseph High School in Westchester, Illinois in 1979 and then immediately went on to represent the U.S. in the Pan America Games in Puerto Rico. That same year, he joined the Indiana Hoosiers basketball team, which at the time was coached by Bobby Knight. In 1981, Thomas led the Hoosiers to the NCAA title.

As the #2 pick in the 1981 NBA Draft, Thomas joined the Detroit Pistons as point guard, one of the smallest, but most powerful players in his position. He brought to the court an edgy and even "physical" spirit that was at times considered "scrappy," and hence was part of the group dubbed the "Bad Boys" of Detroit.

Thomas started in the 1982 All-Star Game for the Eastern Conference, which resulted in him making the All-Rookie team. In 1984, the Pistons faced off with the New York Knicks in the play-offs. In the fifth game, Thomas came back from a disappointing performance in the fourth quarter to score 16 points in one minute

and 33 seconds, which sent the game into overtime. The same type of display could be seen during game six of the 1987 finals against the LA Lakers. Thomas continued to play despite a twisted ankle and single-handedly scored 25 points in just one quarter. Although the Lakers won the series, his performance was demonstrative of just what type of player Thomas was.

In 1988-89, the Pistons were led by Thomas and fellow teammates to what was at the time a franchise record of 63-19. They played well through the play-offs and went on to win back-to-back championships for the first time in franchise history. The following year, Thomas earned the title of NBA Finals Most Valuable Player due to averaging 27.6 points, 7 assists, and 5.2 rebounds per game in the series. It was due to an injury of his Achilles tendon that forced Thomas' retirement the following May.

Thomas played a total of 979 games in the 13 seasons he played for the Pistons, of which 971 he started. He scored a total of 18,822 points and 3,478 rebounds. He also became the fourth player in NBA history to record more than 9,000 assists with a total of 9,061. Thomas ranks ninth in total steals with 1,861 in his career.

SCOTTIE PIPPEN

Scottie Maurice Pippen was born on September 25, 1965 in Hamburg, Arkansas. After his childhood and high school graduation, Pippen attended the University of Central Arkansas, where at 6'1" Pippen was a walk-on for the NAIA school. He grew dramatically over the course of his four-year college career to a height of 6'7" and improved his game so much that he was a viable draft prospect by his senior year. Pippen was selected fifth overall in the 1987 NBA Draft by the Seattle SuperSonics and then immediately was traded to the Chicago Bulls.

Pippen joined the Chicago Bulls as a force to be reckoned with. It was in 1992 that Pippen bloomed into a defensive stopper and a threat on offense for the Bulls. As a small forward, Pippen helped Michael Jordan lead the Bulls to the eastern conference semi-finals for the first time in more than a decade. Continuing to improve, Pippen and the Bulls made the conference finals the following two years, (1991 and 1992). In 1993 Michael Jordan retired unexpectedly from the league, which forced Pippen out into the spotlight for the first time on his own. And in 1994 he earned

the all star game MVP honor for scoring an average of 22 points, 8.7 rebounds, 5.6 assists, 2.9 steals, 0.9 three pointers, and 0.8 blocks per game, all while shooting 49.1 per cent from the field and 32 per cent from the three-point line. He also earned the first of three all NBA first team considerations.

In the 1994-95 season, Michael Jordan announced he would return to the Bulls for another season. He returned and helped the Bulls to a 13-4 record. Pippen led the Bulls in every category including assists, points, rebounds, steals, and blocks, making him one of only five players in NBA history to do so. The following year the Bulls just missed out on their chance of winning 70 games when they lost the two final games of the season. However, they won the title and went on to capture it again the following year in 1996-97 and again in 1997-98, making it their second hat-trick. With his help, the Bulls competed in six NBA championships from 1990 to 1998.

Having battled with General Manager Jerry Krause for number of years, it all finally came to a head when Pippen was traded to the Huston rockets for the 1998-99 season. W

SCOTTIE PIPPEN

disappointment to fans, his trade to the rockets formed one of the best front lines in NBA history by placing together Pippen, Hakeem Olajuwon, and Charles Barkley. The chemistry between the three players was not what it should have been and Pippen was soon traded to the Portland Trail blazers. He played several more seasons with Portland until he re-signed with the Bulls in 2002-03. He retired after the 2003-04 season. To this day Pippen

holds NBA records for the most assists by a forward, steals by a forward in his career, and steals in the play-offs and career. Pippen recorded 20 career triple-doubles, and was the Bulls' career leader in three-point field goals made with 664, three-point field goals attempted with 2,031, and personal fouls with 2,534. Pippen is also one of only three players to make so many appearances in play-off games.

KARL MALONE

Karl Anthony Malone was born on July 24, 1963 in Bernice, Louisiana. After growing up in Summerfield, Louisiana, Malone attended Louisiana Tech University where he played basketball for the school team and led in both scoring and rebounding each of the three seasons he played. It was there that he earned his nickname "The Mailman" for his ability to deliver outstanding performances in the face of great pressure.

In the first round of the 1985 NBA Draft, Malone was selected as the 13th overall pick by the Utah Jazz to play in the power forward position. Malone was so powerful management decided to make trades to bring in other powerful players to partner with Malone on the court. By only his second year with the Jazz, Malone had become the offense foundation. It was the powerful duo that was formed between Malone and Stockton that truly defined the backbone of the Jazz in their record setting 1,412 regular-season games two played together. For six consecutive seasons, beginning in 1987-88, Malone averaged at least 27 points per game and 10 rebounds per game. It was greatly because of Malone's talent that the Jazz would cede multiple 50 win seasons in his career.

The Jazz finally breached the play-offs in both 1997 and 1998 but were defeated both times by the Chicago bulls. Maybe out of pure frustration of not yet having won a championship, Malone joined the Los Angeles Lakers, but made it only to the 2004 NBA finals where the Lakers lost to the Detroit Pistons. It was after the 2004-2005 season that Malone decided to retire.

In his career, Malone scored a total of 36,928 points with an average of 25 points per game. This is the second best all-time on a remarkable 0.516 shooting. He also achieved an average of 10.1 rebounds in his career. He also set a record for free throws in seven separate seasons, achieving an NBA record. Still playing well at the age of 40 meant that Malone became the oldest player to log both a triple-double and be part of the starting five in a NBA finals-bound team. He collected a total of two regular-season MVP awards, 11 NBA First Team nominations, and three selections to the NBA All-Defensive Team. In addition to his many other great feats, Malone holds the record for the all-time most defensive rebounds and is the second all-time on the NBA career scoring list.

126

PAUL ARIZIN

P aul Joseph Arizin was born on April 9, 1928 in Philadelphia, Pennsylvania. He attended La Salle High School but failed to make the basketball team in his senior year and therefore did not play ball until he made the team as a high-scoring forward at Villanova in his sophomore year. During one game in 1949, Arizin scored a total of 85 points against the opposing team. He continued to progress so rapidly that in 1950, he was named the collegiate player of the year, having led the nation in 25.3 points per game.

Arizin was selected by the Philadelphia Warriors as their first pick in the 1950 NBA Draft. He led the league in 1951-52 as the scoring champion. He was most famous for his line-drive jump shots. It may come as a surprise, but Arizin was also the first to ever shoot a jump shot. He teamed up with Neil Johnson to form one of the best offensive duos in the NBA during his era. Arizin averaged 25.4 points a game and 11.3 rebounds on average. "Pitchin' Paul" as he quickly became known, Arizin also held the record for over 40 years as the player who remained in a game for the longest period of time at 63 minutes.

Having sat out the 1952-53 and 1953-54 seasons due to military service during the Korean War, Arizin led the league again scoring champion in the 1956-57 season. That same year, the Warriors went on to achieve the 1956 NBA title. In his career with the Warriors, Arizin played in a total of 10 NBA All-Star games and was chosen as the All-Star MVP in 1952. He was also named to the All-NBA First Team in three separate years.

Having spent his entire professional career with the Philadelphia Warriors, Arizin made the choice to retire from the NBA rather than move with the Warriors to San Francisco. At the time of his retirement he had the third highest career point total in the NBA of 16,266, and no other player had a higher scoring average per game. His record would remain undefeated until 1965.

Arizin was inducted into the basketball hall of fame in 1978. Later, in 1996, Arizin was added to the list of the league's 50 greatest players. Arizin passed away in his sleep at the age of 78 on December 12, 2006, in Springfield, Pennsylvania.

CLYDE DREXLER

Clyde Austin Drexler was born on June 22, 1962 in New Orleans, Louisiana. Drexler graduated from Ross Sterling High School in Huston, Texas in 1980. From there he attended the University of Houston, where he joined players such as Hakeem Olajuwon and Larry Micheaux to form the basketball fraternity known as "Phi Slama Jama," a nickname given to them for their ability to slam dunk and above the rim play. Drexler himself was not considered a great shooter, but had the ability to finish a play with power. While playing for the cougars, Drexler made appearances in two consecutive Final Four series.

After college, Drexler was selected 14th overall in the 1983 NBA Draft to playing for the Portland Trail Blazers. Drexler had an amazing speed and agility on the court. This coupled with his laid back demeanor made him a likable teammate. He also developed his ability to shoot and has a reputation as an effective post player. In addition, his agility gave him the uncanny ability for leaping to make a basket, earning him the name "Clyde the Glide." Developing into a versatile player Drexler was among the leaders in his position in points, rebounds, assists, and steals. He joins only two other players in NBA history to

post career totals of at least 20,000 points, 6000 rebounds, and 6000 assists. He continues to lead guards with his average of offensive rebounds.

In 1990 and again in 1992, Drexler was also selected to join the NBA Finals. Drexler also finished second in voting only to Michael Jordan as MVP in 1991-1992. On February 14, 1995 Drexler was traded on request to the Houston Rockets. Drexler was reunited with former team member and long time friend Hakeem Olajuwon, and together helped the Rockets win the 1995 NBA title. Drexler stayed with the rockets for a total of three additional seasons before retiring after the 1997-98 season to become a head coach at the University of Houston. Upon his retirement Drexler had a number of accomplishments under his belt. These included, a ten-time NBA All-Star, a first team NCAA All-American in 1993, the Southwest Conference Player of the Year in 1983, and All-NBA First Team member in 1992, a two-time All-NBA Second Team member, and a two-time All-NBA Third Team member.

made it to the U.S. Olympics basketball team, the "Dream Team," and won the gold medal. In the regular season, Drexler

130

WALT FRAZIER

Walter "Clyde" Frazier was born March 29, 1945 in Atlanta, Georgia. Frazier attended Howard High School, an all-black racially segregated school in the south. He played both football and baseball on the school teams, but had to learn about basketball on a dirt playground. After high school Frazier attended Southern Illinois University where he accepted an offer to play basketball for Southern Illinois University Carbondale, turning down a football scholarship in the process

He was a master on the court and was named a division two All-American in 1964 and 1965. In 1965 he also led SIU to the NCAA Division II tournament. Unfortunately, in 1966 he became ineligible to play basketball due to academic restrictions. He came back the following season to play point guard and SIU won the national invitation tournament, earning Frazier title of MVP.

Frazier was the fifth pick in the 1967 NBA Draft by the New York Knicks. At that time, Frazier chose to be called Clyde because of his affinity with the movie "Bonnie and Clyde." He had a slow start, averaging only 9.0 points in 1967-68. In an interview with Sport Magazine, Frazier said, "My rookie year, I really played lousy at first." It was actually the new coach, William "Red" Holzman, who came in and found out that Frazier was an aggressive defense. The rookie's playing time soared, as did his confidence. That year he was named in the NBA All-Rookie Team. Frazier's ability to steal the ball turned this practice into an art form. He was always able to surprise the offense with sudden moves and attacks. Frazier was an NBA All-Star seven times. He was also a member of the All-NBA First Team four times, the All-NBA Second Team two times, and the All-Defensive First Team seven times. Frazier is credited with helping the Knicks to capture NBA Championship titles in both 1970 and 1973.

Right before the 1977-78 season, the Knicks traded in Frazier to the Cleveland Cavaliers, ending one of the most fabulous careers in the Knicks history. On his departure, he held franchise records in a number of different categories including: the most games (759), minutes played (28,995), field goals attempted (11,669), field goals made (5,736), free throws attempted (4,017), free throws made (3,145), assists (4,791), and points (14,617).

GEORGE GERVIN

George Gervin was born on April 27, 1952 in Detroit Michigan. He played basketball in college at Eastern Michigan University. He earned the nickname "Iceman" for his cool demeanor on the court. He also earned a reputation as an effective scorer. After leaving college Gervin began his professional basketball career with the ABA's Virginia Squires in 1973. He was signed without the officials even seeing him play due to a rumor that Gervin had made 22 of 25 three-point attempts. In his first year, he made the ABA All-Rookie team in 1973, which he followed up with two All-Star Second Team elections in 1975 and 1976. He was traded to the San Antonio Spurs in 1974, but the team didn't become an official member of the NBA until 1976. Gervin would remain with the Spurs until 1985.

Gervin earned his first scoring crown in 1978, which became one of the most memorable moments in NBA history as he defeated David Thompson by seven hundredths of a point, which Gervin maintained by scoring 63 points in the last game of the season. He was a powerful scorer, leading the NBA in three consecutive seasons from 1978 to 1980 and again in 1982. In fact,

Gervin earned the highest number of scoring titles of any guard in league history prior to Michael Jordan. In 1980 Gervin was also named the NBA All-Star Game MVP.

Probably most notable was Gervin's finger roll. Many others would try to mimic this technique but Gervin could finger roll from as far as the free throw line.

Gervin continued to play for the Spurs until the 1985-86 season, when he left to join the Chicago Bulls. That would be his final season before leaving the NBA. After leaving, Gervin played for several years in Europe including the Banco Roma team in Italy and the Spanish National Basketball League.

During his time with the Spurs, Gervin had become the leader in field goals with 9,201, field goal attempts with 18,111, and points (23,602). Only Wilt Chamberlain and Michael Jordan have won more scoring titles than Gervin, who earned four and he was the only guard ever to win three consecutive titles. For his career, Gervin played in 791 games, scored 20,708 points with an average of 26.2 points per game, 2,214 assists with 2.8 assists per game, and a total of 941 steals.

MOSES MALONE

Moses Eugene Malone was born on March 23, 1955 in Petersburg, Virginia. Malone attended Petersburg high school and immediately after became the first player to go straight from high school into the professional leagues as he joined ABA in 1974. In his first two seasons, Malone achieved averages of 17.2 points and 12.9 rebounds per game. However, the ABA dissolved just after the 1975-76 season. Luckily, the NBA acquired four of the teams and many of the players, wherein the Portland Trail Blazers selected Malone as their fifth overall pick.

He never played for the blazers as he was quickly traded prior to the 1976-77 season to the Buffalo Braves. Yet again, Malone was required to move when after only two games he was traded to the Houston Rockets. This is where he made his name as a fierce rebounder. After completing the combined season for Buffalo and Houston, Malone averaged 13.2 points and 13.1 rebounds per game and was ranked third in rebounding in the NBA, establishing a new NBA record for offensive rebounds in a single season.

In the 1978-79 season, Malone was awarded the NBA MVP award having achieved an average of 24.8 points and 17.6 rebounds. He was named a member of the All-NBA First Team and All-Defensive Second Team. In his fourth season Malone averaged 25.8 points and 14.5 rebounds, which rank and fifth in the league in scoring and second in rebounds. That pushed him to his third consecutive All-Star appearance, which also happened to be his second straight as a starter. At the end of the season he was named in the All-NBA Second Team.

Malone recorded a string of five straight seasons leading the league in rebounding with 14.8 rebounds per game an in 80 appearances. This performance earned him his second straight position on the All-NBA Second Team. In his last season in Houston, Malone and the Rockets appeared in the NBA finals in 1981 immediately followed by a first round play-off exit in 1982. Malone was traded to the 76ers on September 15 where the likes of players such as Julius Erving, Bobby Jones, and Andrew Toney, made it possible to achieve an NBA championship title. Malone led the league in rebounding for a third straight year with an average of 15.3 rebounds per game. He then achieved the same feat for a fourth time in the 1983-84 season with 13.4 rebounds per game. With a 22.7 scoring average, Malone was again named to the All-NBA Second Team and was

MOSES MALONE

Milwaukee Bucks, and San Antonio Spurs.

Looking back over his extensive list of accomplishments, it is near impossible to distinguish Malone's most notable moment. However, here are just a few:

Played more seasons (21) than any other player.

First player in the history to garner five straight rebounding titles after the 1984-1985 season.

Did not foul out during the last 1,212 games—games played the longest streak played without a disqualification.

selected as a member of the NBA all star game for seven consecutive years which he missed due to an ankle injury.

After the 1985-86 season Malone was traded to the Washington Bullets where he earned a place on the All-NBA Second Team. He also scored his 20,000th point in the NBA on April 12, 1986. In his 12th season, Malone recorded 55 double-doubles in one year and ranks fourth in rebounds and 19th in scoring, earning an 11th straight All-Star selection. He would go on as a free agent to play with three more teams over the next eight years, including the Atlanta Hawks,

KEVIN MCHALE

Kevin Edward McHale was born on December 19, 1957, in Hibbing, Minnesota. His father, Paul Austin McHale, was part-Irish American, and his mother, Josephine Patricia Starcevich, was a Croatian-American. Playing basketball in high school, McHale was named Minnesota's Mr. Basketball of 1976. Participating in the AA Minnesota State championship game, his team finished in the runner-up position. McHale earned a position in the Minnesota State high school league hall of fame in 1992.

McHale went on to play the position of power forward for the University of Minnesota where he averaged 15.2 points and 8.5 rebounds per game in the years from 1976 to 1980. He was named to All-Big 10 in 1979 and 1980. McHale still ranks second in the school's history in career points with 1,704 and rebounds with 950. McHale would later be recognized at the university's 100th anniversary as the top player in the history of men's basketball.

McHale was picked by the Celtics in the 1980 NBA Draft as the third overall. McHale was known for his long arms and strong agility on the court. He joined what would later be known as the "Big Three," through an alliance with Larry Bird and Robert Parish. McHale earned the title of NBA's All-Rookie first team during his first season and helped the Celtics record their best year ever in the NBA. From there, the "Big Three" helped take the Celtics in 1981, 1984, and 1986, to the NBA championships. McHale also went on to win the NBA Sixth Man of the Year Award in both 1984 and 1985. In a game against the Clippers in 1985, McHale set his career best in rebounds with a total of 18.

McHale produced some of his best performance during the 1986-87 season. He had become so good at the game that commentators often referred to his performance on the court as the "torture chamber," as defenders were picked off one by one. He set his own record for scoring with 26.1 points, in rebounding with 9.9 per game. McHale shot a total of 60.4 per cent from the field, making him the first player in the NBA's history to shoot 60 per cent or better. He also shot an 83.6 per cent from the free-throw line, becoming the first player to shoot 80 per cent or better. Midway through the season in nine

KEVIN MCHALE

straight games, McHale averaged 30.7 points and 10 rebounds while shooting 71.7 per cent from the floor per game.

During game six of the Eastern Conference Finals, McHale helped protect a one-point lead against the 76ers when he blocked a shot and claimed the rebound with 16 seconds left. The Celtics went on to capture their championship in the NBA Finals. It was after the season that the Celtics earned the title as one of the greatest teams in the history of the NBA. McHale continued to lead the league in field goal percentage in both 1987 and 1988. He shot 60.4 per cent each season. McHale played with the Celtics until 1993,

after which the Celtics retired his #32 jersey.

McHale participated in a total of seven National Basketball Association All-Star Games between 1984 and 1991. He was also selected as a member of the NBA All-Defensive First or Second Team a total of six times. McHale set the record for the most blocked shots with a total of nine in one game, which he accomplished twice. He played 971 regular season games and averaged 17.9 points and 7.3 rebounds. He was recognized as a member of the Basketball Hall of Fame in 1999, and was named as one of the 50 greatest players in the NBA in 1996.

DAVID ROBINSON

David Maurice Robinson was born on August 6, 1965 in Key West, Florida. His family has settled in Woodbridge, Virginia where Robinson played and did well in many sports, except basketball. At a tiny 5'9" tall in junior high, Robinson tried basketball but did not pursue it at that time. However, as a senior at Osbourn Park High School in Manassas, Virginia, Robinson had grown to 6'7" tall, making him the perfect candidate for the high school basketball team. Despite the fact he had never played organized ball, Robinson earned all-area and all-district honors. This didn't seem to peek his interest as he continued to pursue his education over sports, attending the United States Naval Academy for college.

Robinson received the MVP trophy in 1995. In 1996, he was also added to the list of the 50 greatest players in the NBA. However, the spurs had yet to win an NBA championship with Robinson on the team. That all changed during the 1998-99 season. A shortened season due to the league lockout, this season did not officially start until February, shortening the season to only 50 games. It was that season that the Spurs beat the New York Knicks and won the NBA Championship.

In 2003, Robinson announced his retirement, effective at the end of the season. It was only appropriate that the spurs would capture another NBA Championship with Robinson's help. He scored 13 points and 17 rebounds during that game, his final as a professional.

In his career, Robinson averaged a total of 21.1 points, 10.7 rebounds, three blocks, and 2.5 assists per game. He is the only player in the history of the NBA to win in all of the following categories: rebounding, blocked shots, scoring, rookie of the year, defensive player of the year, and most valuable player. Robinson scored more than 20,000 points in his career, making him a member of an elite group. His 10,497 rebounds and 2,954 blocked shots rank him in first place above anyone else wearing a Spurs jersey. He is one of only four players to record a quadruple-double with a total of 34 points, 10 rebounds, 10 assists, and 10 blocks.

BILL RUSSEL

William Felton "Bill" Russel was born on February 12, 1934 in Monroe, Louisiana. Due to a number of race-related issues, Russell's family moved to Oakland, California when he was only eight. With a passion for playing, Russell adamantly practiced his basketball skills. He would not truly come into his own as a player until his junior year in high school at McClymonds in Oakland.

Turning down an opportunity to play for the Globetrotters, Russell was drafted by the Boston Celtics in the 1956 NBA draft. Due to an Olympic commitment, Russell did not join the Celtics until December of 1956, playing only 48 games in that season. But he averaged 14.7 points and a league high of 19.6 rebounds per game. In game one of the play-offs that year Russell finished with 16 points and 31 rebounds as well as seven blocks, and the Celtics went on to make an appearance in the NBA Finals. It was in game seven of the finals wherein he blocked an attempted shot by Jack Coleman to protect the narrow Celtics win of 103-102. The Celtics won their first NBA championship that season. The following season Russell averaged a

total of 16.6 points and 22.7 rebounds per game. He received the honour of the NBA's most valuable player, but oddly enough was only named as a member of the Second Team. The Celtics won the NBA Title yet again in 1959. It was in the following season that Russell would develop a legendary rivalry with another great player, Wilt Chamberlain. Meeting the Warriors in the Eastern Division finals, Russell and Chamberlain went head to head and the Celtics scored a 4-2 series win. In 1965, Russell became the highest paid NBA player, making US$1.00 more than Chamberlain.

After 13 years of playing for the Celtics, Bill Russell retired. He had reached the NBA Championships 11 out of 13 years and was selected as the NBA MVP five times. Russell made the All-NBA First Team three times, the All-NBA Second Team eight times, and the NBA All-Defensive Team once. He was a 12 time NBA All-Star from 1958-69 and an Olympic gold medalist in 1956. His #6 jersey was retired by the Celtics in 1972 and Russell was inducted into the Basketball Hall of Fame in 1975. He was listed as one of the greatest NBA players in history in 1996.

BILL WALTON

William Theodore Walton, III (Bill) was born on November 5th, 1952, in San Diego, California. It was in the fourth grade that Walton learned about the game of basketball from his Coach Rocky Graziano.

After high school, Walton enrolled at UCLA in 1970 where he played center for the freshman team.

Walton was picked number one overall in the 1974 NBA draft by the Portland Trailblazers. Walton suffered injury his first two years and therefore did not have a strong seasons until 1976-77. It was that year that Walt led the NBA in rebounds and blocks per game. Consequently, he was named in the NBA's First-All Defensive Team and All-NBA Second Team. The trail blazers went on to win the NBA Title in 1977 due in large part to Walton's performance for which he earned the title of Finals MVP.

The following year, the Blazers won 50 of their first 60 games. Walton was named as the league MVP and played his only All-Star game that same year. He was also selected for the NBA's First All -Defensive Team and All-NBA First Team. Due to ethical reasons, Walton decided to sit out the 1978-79 season in protest

until he could become a free agent the following year. It was at that time that he joined the San Diego Clippers. He sat the bench for the majority of the time he was with the Clippers due to injury. It wasn't until 1985 when Walton joined the Boston Celtics that he once again experienced the feeling of playing in the NBA championship and winning. He also was able to realize his childhood dream of playing for the Celtics.

For his contribution to the game and support of fellow players, Kevin McHale and Robert Parish, Walton earned the honour of being named the NBA's Sixth Man Award that year. He was the only player who ever won a NBA Final, the Sixth Man Award and Most Valuable Player.

Walton is the second of only four players to lead the league in both block shots in rebounding in the same season. After his retirement, his #32 jersey was retired in 1989. Walton was inducted into the Oregon Sports Hall of Fame in 1993. In 1997, the Basketball Hall of Fame in 1995 and into Walton was also inducted into the national high school sports hall of fame. This made him the first male basketball player from the state of California to receive such an honour.

JERRY WEST

Jerry Alan West was born on May 28, 1938 in Cheylan, West Virginia. West was a phenomenal basketball player in high school where he played at East Bank High from 1952 to 1956. He was the first high school player to score more than 900 points in a single season, earning him the title of West Virginia Player of the Year. He was subsequently named an All-State from 1953-56 and was an All-American in 1956. West had such an impact of the school, that for one day a year, the school is officially called West Bank High.

After graduation West attended West Virginia University Mountaineers from 1956 to 1960. As a sophomore, West scored an average of 17.8 points and and 11.1 rebounds per game, while shooting 49.6 per cent from the field with a 73.2 per cent average from the free-throw line. In his college career, West totaled 2,309 points and 1,240 of rebounds, averaging 24.8 points and 13.3 rebounds per game, ranking him in first place for the most points scored, most points per game, most field goals made, most free-throws attempted, most rebounds, most double-doubles, most 20-point games, and most 30-point games. West was drafted by the Los Angeles Lakers as the second overall pick in the 1960

NBA Draft. During the 1969-70 season, West led the league in scoring. It was during game three of the NBA Finals that year that West hit a 60 foot shot on the buzzer, and pushed the game into overtime. This shot has become known as one of the most memorable moments in Finals history. The Lakers lost that game which is a shame, because had the shot counted for 3 points as it does today, then they would have won.

During the 1971-72 season, West led the league in assists. It was during that same season that West and the Lakers won 33 straight games as well as their first championship. West made appearances in nine Finals series in his career. At that time, steals were not recorded by the NBA. It was not until his final season that West became the first player in the NBA to record 10 steals in one game, a record which he still holds for the franchise.

West announced his retirement in 1974. Throughout his career, West scored 25,192 points, averaged 27 points per game, and made 7,160 free-throws, as well as 6,238 assists. He had made the NBA All-Defensive First Team four times and the All-NBA First Team 10 times.

150

JAMES WORTHY

James Ager Worthy was born February 27, 1961 in Gastonia, North Carolina. He played basketball at Ashbrook High School where he averaged 21.5 points and 12.5 rebounds in his senior year. As early as the ninth grade, Worthy's performance on the talent was making front-page news. After graduation, Worthy performed as an outstanding basketball player and crucial team member for the University of North Carolina. He was the leading scorer with 15.6 points per game on average. Playing against Michael Jordan's team in the 1982 Play-off's, Worthy stole the ball and led the team to victory. For his performance during that game, including scoring 28 points, he was named the most outstanding player.

In the 1982 NBA draft, Worthy was the first overall pick of the Los Angeles Lakers. He immediately started making headlines with his 13.4 points on average per game and 0.579 field goal percentage, a Laker rookie record. Worthy made a name for himself as a small forward, one of the best baseline post players with a dynamic turnaround jump-shot. Playing another basketball great, Magic Johnson, Worthy leveraged his own talent for scoring, with Johnson's passing ability. He also became well-known for his trademark move—the one-handed swoop dunk.

He made the 1983 All-Rookie First Team. In 1985, 1987 and 1988, the Lakers went to the NBA championships with Worthy's help, and he led the team in play-off scoring in both 1987 and 1988. In game seven of the 1988 NBA Finals, Worthy scored 28 points and nine rebounds. Following, in game seven, he scored 36 points, 16 rebounds, and 10 assists, recording a triple - double. It was his first, and arguably his best. It was because of this performance that Worthy earned the award for most valuable player. Worthy went on to lead his team in scoring during regular season games in 1990-91 and 1991-92. It is no surprise that Worthy was a seven-time NBA All-Star.

Worthy announced his retirement in November of 1994. He had played professional basketball for 12 seasons. He had been noted as an All-Star of the NBA a total of seven times. He is probably best known as "Big Game James" for the 926 NBA games he played, scoring an average of 17.6 points per game, 5.1 rebounds, and leading as the fifth all-time in team scoring with 16,320 points. His post-

JAMES WORTHY

season career averages were even higher than the regular season games with 21.1 points and 5.2 rebounds per game. He is the second all-time in team steals with 1,041, and is the sixth all-time in team field goal percentage with 0.521. Worthy was added to the list of the top 50 NBA players of all time in 1996 and was later inducted into the Naismith Memorial Basketball Hall of Fame in 2003. He is one of only seven retired Los

Angeles Lakers to have his jersey retired, #42.

According to the NBA Encyclopedia, "Worthy will be remembered for his breathtaking athletic skills—the blinding speed, the smooth, effortless glides to the hoop, the one-handed tomahawk jams. And he will be recalled as the ultimate clutch player—his career post-season field goal percentage of .544 ranks among the top 10 on the NBA's all-time play-off list."

DIRK NOWITZKI

Nowitzki decided to declare for the 1998 NBA Draft at the age of 20. He had a promise from Boston Celtics head coach Rick Pitino that his team would take him with the 10th overall selection. However, one other team was interested in the German prospect: the Dallas Mavericks, and they selected him just one pick earlier. The Mavericks also got the draft rights to nineteenth-overall pick Pat Garrity, but that same draft, Garrity was traded (along with other players and future draft considerations) to the Phoenix Suns for young point guard Steve Nash. On that night, the Dallas Mavericks acquired two of the pieces on which they would build their franchise for years to come.

Mavs GM Don Nelson touted Nowitzki as the sure-fire 1998-99 Rookie of the Year at the draft, a lofty expectation for a 20-year-old who was in the U.S. for the first time. Dallas fans were understandably upset, then, when Nowitzki looked lost when on the floor in mop-up minutes as a rookie. Determined to prove that he could be a force in the NBA, Nowitzki returned to Germany in the 1999 off-season, working hard on sharpening his total game. The summer of work helped immensely, as Nowitzki emerged as a starter and future star in 1999-2000, when he averaged 17.5 points, 6.5 rebounds, and 2.5 assists, finishing second in voting for the league's Most Improved Player.

The following season 2000-01, he averaged 21.8 points and 9.2 rebounds and became the first Maverick to be named to the All-NBA Team, making the third team.

ANDREW GAZE

Andrew Gaze, born July 24, 1965 in Melbourne, Victoria is Australia's best known basketball player, and undoubtedly one of its most successful.

Son of Australian basketball stalwart Lindsay Gaze, Andrew began a stellar career in the NBL at age 18, being named Rookie of the year in 1984. His incredible shooting skills saw him become the top scorer in the league for a total of 14 seasons. Gaze combined a great three-point shot with an equally good pass. A crowd favourite, one of Gaze's trademark plays was a pass to American import Lanard Copeland for an alley oop. Playing under his father with the Melbourne Tigers, Gaze led the team to two titles and were perpetual finalists.

Gaze also excelled at the international arena, playing in a total of five Olympic Games with the Boomers and led them to their best performance, fourth at the 1996 Summer Olympics. He was selected as flag bearer for the Australian team at the opening ceremony at the Sydney 2000 Games. He is the scoring record holder in Olympic competition, and second-highest scorer of all-time in World Championship play.

In 1989 Gaze played a season of U.S. college basketball at Seton Hall, where his team made the 1989 NCAA finals, losing in overtime to

158

He tried out with the NBA's Seattle SuperSonics, but was not offered a contract and ultimately waived. In 1993-94 he played seven games for the Washington Bullets. He had another short stint in the NBA in lockout-shortened 1998-99 with the San Antonio Spurs, but received very little court time and was injured for the latter part of the season. He received a championship ring after the Spurs won the 1999 NBA title, although he was left off the play-off roster.

Whilst Gaze never had a steady NBA career like Chicago Bulls center Luc Longley, Gaze's superlative domestic record, not to mention an affable personality, fixed him in the public mind as the face of Australian basketball through the 1990s and early 2000s.

After the Sydney Olympics, Gaze retired from international competition, but continued to play in the NBL. On May 12, 2005, he announced his retirement from the game after 612 games in the NBL and 20 years as a professional basketballer.

He is known for his gentle, unflappable nature, prematurely grey hair and reticence to slam dunk. Today, Gaze has carved out a career as a media personality commentating NBL basketball matches for SEN 1116 and Fox Sports.

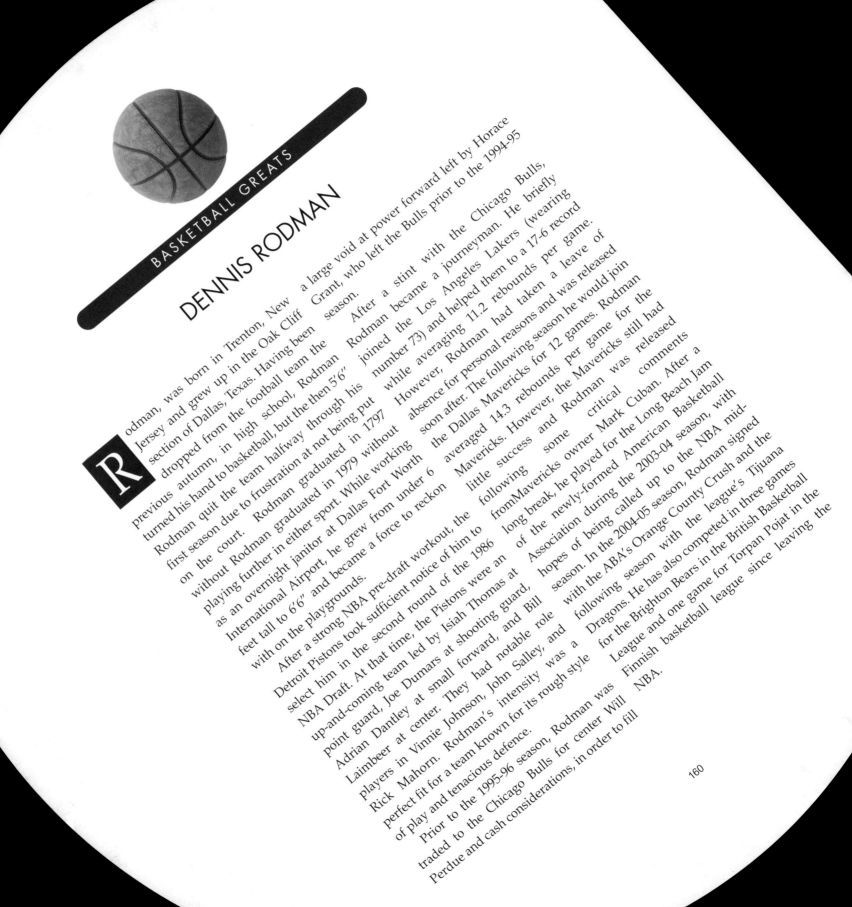

DENNIS RODMAN

Rodman, was born in Trenton, New Jersey and grew up in the Oak Cliff section of Dallas, Texas. Having been dropped from the football team the previous autumn, in high school, Rodman turned his hand to basketball, but the then 5'6" Rodman quit the team halfway through his first season due to frustration at not being put on the court. Rodman graduated in 1979 without Rodman graduated in 1797 playing further in either sport. While working as an overnight janitor at Dallas Fort Worth International Airport, he grew from under 6 feet tall to 6'6" and became a force to reckon with on the playgrounds.

After a strong NBA pre-draft workout, the Detroit Pistons took sufficient notice of him to select him in the second round of the 1986 NBA Draft. At that time, the Pistons were an up-and-coming team led by Isiah Thomas at point guard, Joe Dumars at shooting guard, Adrian Dantley at small forward, and Bill Laimbeer at center. They had notable role players in Vinnie Johnson, John Salley, and Rick Mahorn. Rodman's intensity was a perfect fit for a team known for its rough style of play and tenacious defence. Prior to the 1995-96 season, Rodman was traded to the Chicago Bulls for center Will Perdue and cash considerations, in order to fill

a large void at power forward left by Horace Grant, who left the Bulls prior to the 1994-95 season.

After a stint with the Chicago Bulls, Rodman became a journeyman. He briefly joined the Los Angeles Lakers (wearing number 73) and helped them to a 17-6 record while averaging 11.2 rebounds per game. However, Rodman had taken a leave of absence for personal reasons and was released soon after. The following season he would join the Dallas Mavericks for 12 games. Rodman averaged 14.3 rebounds per game for the Mavericks. However, the Mavericks still had little success and Rodman was released following some critical comments from Mavericks owner Mark Cuban. After a long break, he played for the Long Beach Jam of the newly-formed American Basketball Association during the 2003-04 season, with hopes of being called up to the NBA mid-season. In the 2004-05 season, Rodman signed with the ABA's Orange County Crush and the following season with the league's Tijuana Dragons. He has also competed in three games for the Brighton Bears in the British Basketball League and one game for Torpan Pojat in the Finnish basketball league since leaving the NBA.

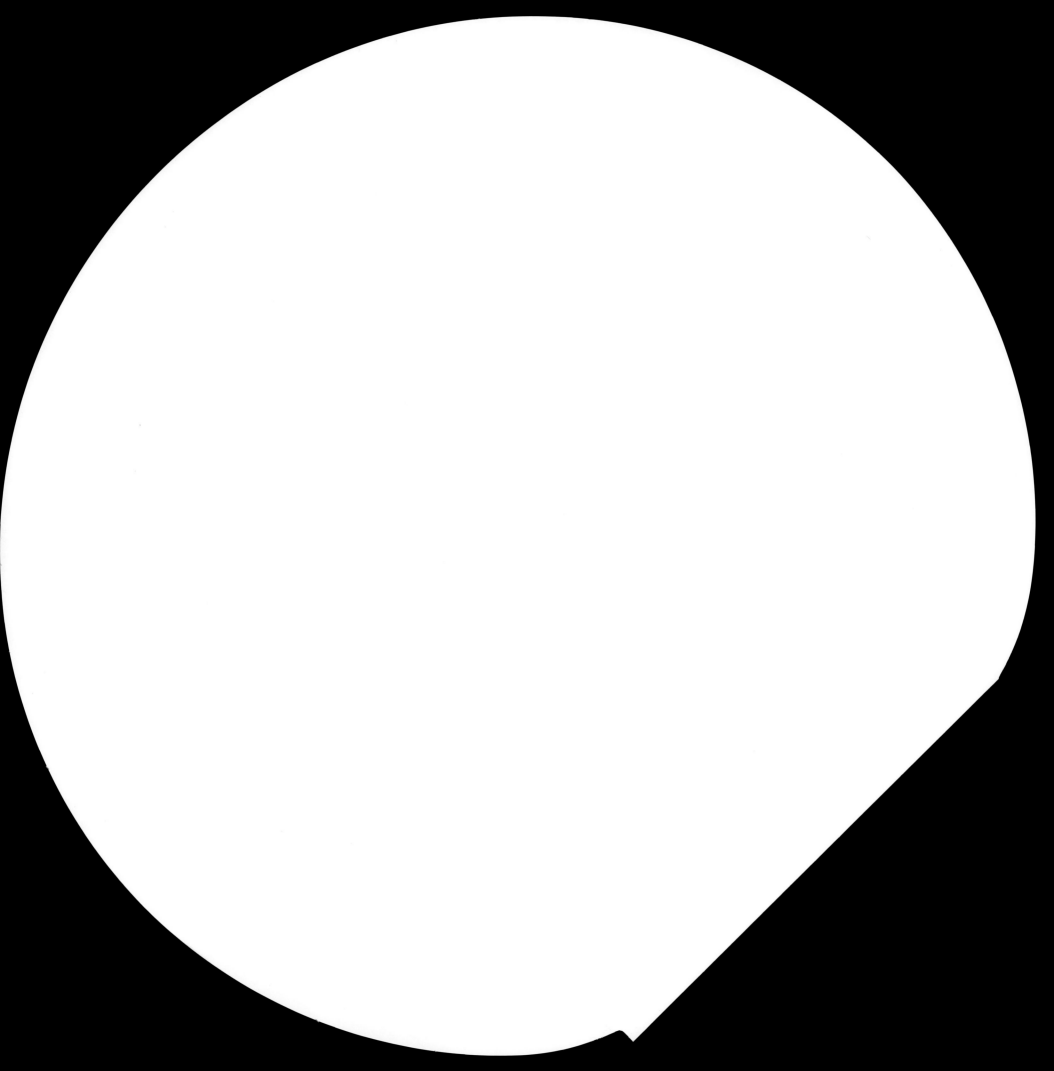

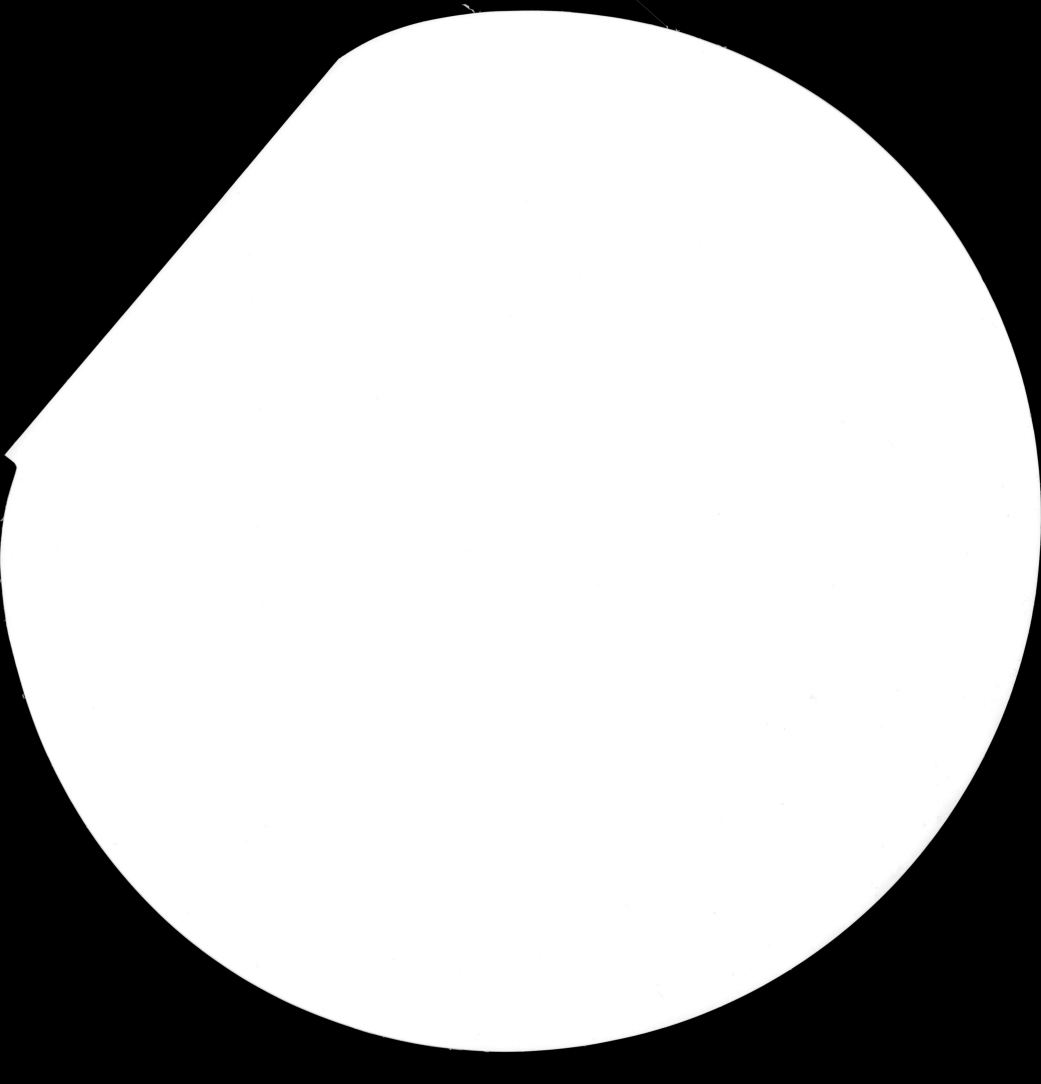